Write Like a Pro

10 Rules To Be a Better Writer

Kalyanaraman Durgadas

An imprint of

Srishti Publishers & Distributors

Srishti Publishers & Distributors
A unit of AJR Publishing LLP
212A, Peacock Lane
Shahpur Jat, New Delhi – 110 049

editorial@srishtipublishers.com

First published by Bold,
an imprint of Srishti Publishers & Distributors in 2025

10 9 8 7 6 5 4 3 2 1

The views expressed in this publication are those of the author alone and should not be taken as expert instructions or commands. While all attempts have been made to verify the information provided in this publication, neither the author nor the publisher assume any responsibility for errors, omissions, or contrary interpretation of the subject matter herein.

Printed and bound in India.

To my mother, the late Abhirami Durgadas

CONTENTS

Introduction

The book is about how to write well and how not to write. Writing is much like sculpting—removing everything that does not contribute to a beautiful finished sculpture. Understanding what not to write significantly enhances your work without affecting your style, tone, or originality.

While it is not possible to list every mistake that writers can commit, I have focused on the errors that are often made by them.

Revisions help your writing come together. Understanding what to avoid is invaluable during this phase. If you keep in mind the various suggestions given in the book, it will help you not only during your revision but also while composing your story or article for the first time.

It is not necessary that you attempt to implement every bit of advice I offer all the time. Hold on to that deliberate intent during the revision process. Over time, you will find that you make fewer mistakes.

The book will also tell you how to fix things that have gone wrong.

I have furnished extensive resources (books, websites, software tools, and, in some cases, podcasts) covering various aspects of writing.

What the book does not cover

The book is not a specific manual for writing fiction or non-fiction. It merely covers the various aspects of good writing (primarily by pointing out the bad ones). In my fifty years of experience in writing, editing, mentoring, and conducting writing workshops for writers, I have encountered and addressed many challenges that are often faced by writers. I have covered these areas in this book. However, neither do I talk about elements of fiction nor directly about theme, story, plot, characterisation, or setting—at least, not in this book.

The book does not specifically encompass academic writing.

It is not a book on grammar. It does not address errors of punctuation.

It covers only those aspects that trouble many writers. You certainly do not need to be a grammar expert to benefit from this book.

Structure of the book

The book is laid out in six parts:

Part 1—The first part, titled 'Write Thus!', explores some of the important aspects of good writing.

Part 2—'Paragraphs and Larger Text' deals with larger blocks of text, now getting into the real business of avoiding bad writing.

Part 3—'Phrases/Sentences' is concerned with smaller chunks, i.e., sentences, including complicated, confusing, ornamented, or ambiguous sentences.

Part 4—'Words, Words!' is all about the building blocks of writing—words—emphasising the avoidance of words that are complex, vague, boring, confusing, incorrect, or inappropriate.

Part 5—'All Together' discusses the overall patterns and structures and the correct approach to writing advice.

Part 6—This includes appendices that augment Part 4. It also lists useful resources for the writer.

Ten Rules to be a Better Writer

There is also a parallel structure. Ten rules that can make you a better writer are illustrated in the first ten chapters. The rules are:

Rule 1: Show Rather Than Tell
Rule 2: Mind Your POV
Rule 3: Let the Dialogue Multitask
Rule 4: Control the Pacing
Rule 5: Make a Scene
Rule 6: Structure Your Narrative
Rule 7: Watch Your Grammar
Rule 8: Avoid Complexity
Rule 9: Mean What You Say
Rule 10: Develop Your Unique Voice.

The ten rules are elaborated in chapters 1-10 respectively.

Rules 6 and 10 are further illustrated in 'Chapter 13: Structure and Patterns' and in 'Chapter 14: Your Standpunkt'.

Suggested reading order

First, read Part 1. Read Parts 2, 3, and 4 in any order. Part 4 has additional information in the appendices. You can look them up either immediately after reading the relevant chapter or at any other time at your leisure.

Read Part 5 to understand the best way to act on or ignore the advice offered in this book (or, for that matter, any writing advice).

Exercises in the book

I have peppered the book generously with examples and exercises, and I recommend that you look through each of them. I do so for a reason. The exercises in the book are not merely meant for testing yourself. Some of them illustrate principles not covered in the main text.

I have suggested answers to the exercises. These are not necessarily the only right answers or the best; your answer may fit better. Please also bear in mind that I am sneaky. A small proportion of the sentences need no correction. So, make corrections only where necessary.

An additional goal of these exercises is to help you commit the principles given in the book to your memory.

Appendices

The appendices in the book list further examples.

The right attitude

There is a lot of writing advice strewn around in the book, and it helps to have the right attitude towards writing advice in general.

Taking writing advice

If you are an inexperienced writer, just follow the advice until you know enough to ignore the advice.

If you are an experienced writer, go ahead and break the rules, but you must have a reason to do so. It could be any of those given below:

- It does not fit your style.
- The intended audience is different.
- The context justifies the breaking of the rule.
- You do not agree (after careful reflection) with what I have suggested.

Do not let 'rules' limit your voice. Let it come through.

The chapter titled 'Standpunkt' addresses the inherent conflicts in writing.

In this book, I have tried to present the rationale behind the rules of writing, and just knowing this should help you make informed decisions about breaking them.

A foreshadowing—summary of the book

As a writer, you should always keep the reader in mind. The reader is king. Avoid writing anything that is likely to:

- confuse the reader
- make him go 'huh?'
- make it difficult for him to understand
- offend him
- bore him

(Before you accuse me of gender bias, let me clarify that I use 'she' and 'her' when I write about an author and 'he' and 'him' when writing about a reader. It is just a random piece of convention that I have followed, though not consistently.)

This translates to writing in a manner that is:

- brief
- active
- clear
- simple

Now, let us continue on to the book.

PART 1:
WRITE THUS!

Chapter 1
Showing, not Telling

Rule 1: Show Rather Than Tell

Introduction

From childhood, we are used to 'telling'. The stories that began with 'Once upon a time', the fairy tales, and the legends from the epics were all told orally. However, they were narrated in interesting ways, with changes in tones, imitation of animal sounds, and dramatic gestures. That kind of telling does not translate easily to print.

As adults, we are also exposed to movies, documentaries, and animations and, in our consumption of stories, we expect a lot of visual content. If we do not get enough fodder for our eyes, we tend to get disengaged from the story.

There is another aspect to it. We need to believe what we are seeing, if only for the moment, in order to identify with it. When we are *told* something, we do not believe it. However, when we *experience* something, even through someone else's eyes, there is a possibility of believing it.

Therefore, if you want your writing to engage the reader, it must allow him to experience, not merely hear. Rather than state conclusions, it should be in a form that holds up evidence, so that the reader can make up his own mind. Since the reader has reached the conclusion himself, he believes.

'Show, don't tell' is a writing technique that allows the reader to experience the story through sensory details, through the expression of emotions and actions.

When the reader infers, it is his conclusion, and he has already bought into it. He believes and identifies.

Let me give you an example—Telling: 'He was hungry.'

Showing: The table creaked with bread, fruits, and jugs of mead. He breathed in the fresh smell of food. His stomach growled. He salivated.

Showing over telling

Vivid and interesting

The descriptions, when you are showing, are more vivid and therefore, more interesting.

In the passage quoted below, Goldman could have simply said, '*Fezzik waited for the man in black with a stone in hand.*' Instead, he wrote:

> *Fezzik glanced down toward the figure racing up the path toward him. Still a good distance away. Time enough to practice. Fezzik picked up a rock the size of a cannonball and aimed at a crack in the mountain thirty yards away.*
>
> *Swoosh.*
>
> *Dead center.*
>
> *He picked up a bigger rock and threw it at a shadow line twice as distant.*
>
> *Not quite swoosh.*
>
> *Two inches to the right.*
>
> *Fezzik was reasonably satisfied. Two inches off would still crush a head if you aimed for the center. He groped around, found a perfect rock for throwing; it just fit his hand. Then he moved to the sharp turn in the path, backed off …*

WILLIAM GOLDMAN, *PRINCESS BRIDE*

Bringing in the senses

Here is an example.

> *Outdoors it is growing dark and cool. The Norwegian maples exhale the smell of their sticky new buds and the broad living-room windows along Wilbur Street show beyond the silver patch of a television set, the warm bulbs burning in kitchens, like fires at the backs of caves. He walks downhill. The day is gathering itself in. He now and then touches with his hand the rough bark of a tree or the dry twigs of a hedge, to give himself the small answer of a texture. At the corner, where Wilbur Street meets Potter Avenue, a mailbox stands leaning in twilight on its concrete post. Tall two-petaled street sign, the cleat-gouged trunk of the telephone pole holding its insulators against the sky, fire hydrant like a golden bush: a grove. He used to love to climb the poles. To shinny up from a friend's*

shoulders until the ladder of spikes came to your hands, to get up to where you could hear the wires sing. Terrifying motionless whisper. It always tempted you to fall, to let the hard spikes in your palms go and feel the space on your back, feel it take your feet and ride up your spine as you fell. He remembers how hot your hands felt at the top, rubbed full of splinters from getting up to where the spikes began. Listening to the wires as if you could hear what people were saying, what all that secret adult world was about.

JOHN UPDIKE, *RUN RABBIT RUN*

Note how Updike connects phrases with various senses:

- 'smell of the sticky buds'—smell
- 'touches with his rough hand'—kinesthetic
- 'holding its insulators against the sky, fire hydrant like a fire bush'—visual
- 'listening to the wires as if you could hear what people were saying'—hearing

Triggering reader emotion

Showing does a much better job of triggering reader emotion, as you can see from the following passage:

> Tears streamed down Jane's face as she watched her house burn to the ground. She stood frozen, unable to move or speak, as flames licked at the windows and smoke billowed into the night sky. All of her possessions, all of her memories, were being destroyed right before her eyes. She couldn't believe this was happening. As the fire trucks arrived and firefighters rushed to extinguish the blaze, Jane collapsed to the ground, sobbing uncontrollably.

Compare this with a bare-bones telling:

> Jane's house burnt down. There was a lot of smoke. The fire-trucks began arriving as Jane fell down crying.

The main purpose of any piece of writing is to keep the reader engaged. Showing engages the reader.

Convincing character development

Showing allows you to develop your fictional characters much more effectively than telling. In my book, *Songs of the Cauvery,* I show Sambu's tendency of mild stinginess through events in multiple places and let the reader arrive at his conclusion. Here is an example.

> *'Jasmine string,' he said, 'Four hand widths.' 'And be careful with your hands, and don't pull to stretch one hand width to two,' he added.*
>
> *The shopkeeper measured out the flowers generously, adding a couple of inches to each width, taking care to keep the string slack. He cut the plantain fibre with which the flowers were tied on the sharp edge of a stone and wrapped them in a leaf and placed the parcel on the counter. Sambu took the package and dropped a quarter-anna coin. The shopkeeper started to protest.*
>
> *'This itself is too much. I will take something else from you later,' said Sambu, and walked away without a glance at the shopkeeper.*
>
> KALYANARAMAN DURGADAS, *SONGS OF THE CAUVERY*

Some issues with showing

Most times, showing lengthens the sentences. In the bargain, you get better reader engagement. For instance, instead of saying 'he was old', you might say:

> His face was deeply lined. His lips were compressed—there were hardly any teeth visible when he opened his mouth. He stooped a little while walking. His hands shook as he moved them to make a point.

If you had described an old man thus in your book, he might linger on in the reader's mind for a while. In case the old man was an unimportant character, never to be seen again, this description is unnecessary. It gives undue importance to a minor character and sets up the reader's expectation that the character would become important later on.

Where do you find telling?

In exposition

The most blatant forms of telling occur in exposition. When the writer is conveying some information or trying to explain something, she feels forced to take recourse to telling. For instance:

He had been waiting at the office since morning, and he was getting tired. Everyone in the room seemed equally bored and equally tired.

In descriptions

Descriptions of people and places often have a fair amount of telling. Describing yourself when you are writing in the first person is problematic. For instance:

I am Ramesh. People call me Ramu for short. I am five feet seven inches tall and weigh about 60 kilos. I like to part my hair in the centre and brush it back.

There are few things uglier than such descriptions, and don't even think about looking into a mirror and describing what you see. *That* is one of those few things that are uglier.

In dialogue

When one person tells something the other already knows, in order to inform the reader, you get the worst form of telling in dialogue.

I swear this is true. I once had to sit through the presentation of a play in which the following lines occurred:

'Ohh, you have stabbed me with a long knife and blood is flowing.'

The dialogue got steadily worse from then on.

In interior monologue or thoughts

The Grand Trunk Express nearly mowed the protagonist over and he thinks, 'Thank God! I escaped.'

A pretty girl leans over unexpectedly and kisses him full on the mouth. 'That was nice,' he thought.

He was upset. Why would such a close friend stab me in the throat with a long knife? What have I done to merit this? I must now take revenge.

Do these thoughts make sense? Don't be that writer.

In action

Large-scale excursions into the telling of a childhood incident tend to disconnect the reader from the action. For instance:

> The man had the point of a sword at the warrior's neck. He (the warrior) remembered how his kid sister would steal up to him behind his back and poke him with a hairpin.

Summarising a relevant action instead of showing it is one of the deadly sins. For instance:

> Four people had surrounded him. He killed all of them. Then three more came up to him. He killed them. Then two more. Luckily, before running through them, he noticed they wore his own regiment's colours. But to be on the safe side, he killed them, too.

The writer has effectively killed the action, too.

Getting showing right

Point of View

For a more complete treatment of Point of View, see the chapter titled 'Point of View'.

First person

If you choose a first-person point of view, automatically, most of your writing will show, not tell. It is also difficult to make a POV mistake in the first person. You will show only what you can see, hear, smell, or feel. For instance, you are not likely to write:

> Just beyond the next hill, out of my sight, a panther crouched in anticipation.
>
> Or,
>
> I did not see two people who came tiptoeing from behind and hit me with an iron shovel. Nor did I hear them say 'here's our victim' in Bhojpuri and laugh.

This is not a recommendation to write only in the first- person POV. There are limitations in the first- person POV that may prove onerous.

Third person, limited

A close third- person point of view is nearly the same as a first-person point of view, except that in the former, you even get to look at the face of the Point of View character.

It is easy to slip out of a third- person POV and start describing others' motivations and feelings.

Let us assume that Joe is the POV character.

Joe socked James on the jaw. It hurt.

You have strayed from the POV. How do you know it hurt?

Being in the character's point of view and staying there is a useful way of ensuring showing. This, however, is not sufficient. For effective showing, make sure you are not filtering actions, thoughts, and words.

Unfiltered

You 'tell' when you hand over thoughts, words, and actions down to the reader, brokering them through filter words. (Please see the section on filter words).

Shown below is a progression from a filtered account to increasing amounts of showing:

- He thought he could see an animal.
- He could see an animal.
- He saw an animal.
- He saw a flatfooted-meredog.
- A flatfooted-meredog scurried past.
- A flatfooted-meredog scurried past, its mouth covered in blood.

The second and third sentences remove the filter words 'thought' and 'could' respectively, and the other sentences use increasingly specific descriptions and eliminate the additional filter of 'saw'.

Vivid language and strong verbs

Use language associated with the senses and strong verbs instead of modifier-verb combinations to enhance the showing.

I have gone a little overboard with this example of using all the senses, but it should give you an idea, anyway.

The scene: The old man was trying to cross the road. I helped him across.

Incorporate sight:

The stick in the man's hand that looked as old as the man himself wavered. He pointed it ahead as though it helped him cross the road, but didn't walk ahead. He looked around. I saw the helplessness in his wrinkled eyes.

Add sound:

He was about to say something, perhaps ask for help to cross the road.

'Can I help, sir?'

His stick came down with a thud, I thought, in relief.

Add smell:

I went nearer. The smell of Old Spice wafted across to me, and I was transported back to my childhood. I remembered my grandfather. I was being lifted as a child, and the smell of Old Spice combined with the tactile sensation of a rough cheek on mine.

Add touch:

His hand shook as it held mine. Thick veins entwined the hand. I held his hand delicately.

Add taste:

I looked up to see the old man's eyes glistening with tears. I felt something trickle down my cheeks as well. It tasted salty.

You get the idea.

You may not always get the best results in one edit pass, as shown. Here is another example of possible progressive edits.

Progressive edits

- He could hear the captain's loud voice over the clattering of the wagons.
- He heard the captain's loud voice over the clattering of the wagons.
- He heard the captain shouting over the clattering of the wagons.
- The captain shouted over the clattering of the wagons.
- The captain shouted over the clatter of the wagons.
- The captain shouted obscenities over the clatter of the wagons.

Ordering (chronological and logical)

The experience of the viewpoint character has to be communicated in a flow, in a continuous stream of experience. A chronological order or a logical order (effect following cause and reaction following action) is best.

Other areas that require telling

Backstory

If the author wants to start the story in the middle of the action, there could be a problem. You have to tell the backstory sometime. This is a real problem because, to ensure engagement, the backstory has to be shown in the scene as though it is happening here and now. You then end up giving undue importance to a prequel that may only be of passing interest to the reader.

You want to keep it short because, for the reader, the past story is something that has already happened. The potential for holding the attention of the reader is low. However, from the author's perspective, it may contain some information that the reader must know in order to follow the story or to understand the motivation of the characters.

You have a few hard choices now.

1. Show the backstory in a scene, anyway. You also need to keep it short, because, well, it is past due.

The reader already knows a couple of things. After the initial scene, the past story loses some of its lustre. When the reader gets to that part, he knows what some characters do after some time elapses, at least to the extent to know which ones will be alive. The backstory, therefore, needs to be kept short. The problem is that when you show rather than tell, you use many more words and increase the probability that it will disengage a reader.

As an author, play the odds.

2. Sometimes, the better solution is to simply 'tell' the story as succinctly as possible and hope that you have not given the reader enough time to get disengaged. If you do it late enough in the story, you may be able to get away with it.

Reveal the backstory as late as possible, just before you need it. This serves many purposes. You allow the momentum of the story to carry the reader through these passages, and the reader invests enough in the story. He will then be loath to throw it away and stop reading.

3. The third solution is to intersperse the backstory in devious ways through the narrative—sometimes, in a piece of dialogue,

sometimes, in a flash of remembrance at an opportune moment by one of the characters. Ensure that the reader does not feel that you have constructed the dialogues artificially just to inform him. Even though you are taking a risk in more places when you distribute the backstory through your work, this is the option that many modern writers prefer.

Other structural choices may ease the situation. For instance, in *A Man called Ove,* Fredrik Backman alternates between the past and the present in alternate chapters, giving the past and the present equal importance. The brilliant contrast between what the main character was and what he appears to be at present carries the story through.

Or, you could tell the entire story chronologically, like I have done in *Songs of the Cauvery*.

It is clear from the above choices that none of them is wholly satisfactory. Well, I never said that being an author is easy.

Transitions

Authors provide transitions when they want to take excursions in time and place. These transitions are particularly important when you want to show a scene from the past.

In writing, you cannot have the cinematic techniques of 'fades' and 'dissolves'. The effect can be achieved using a paragraph break, a scene break, a mention of a date or a significant event from the past, a showing of the state of mind.

The transitions to a future date could be short, as in 'one year later', 'the next day', or it could be a longer narrative summary of what happened in-between. It could even be:

> *But from a narrative point of view, in 105 pages, nothing happens. Except this: 'What with one thing and another, three years passed.'*
>
> WILLIAM GOLDMAN, *THE PRINCESS BRIDE*

The modern reader, brought up on a steady diet of visual stimuli—and fast-changing ones at that—hardly needs transitions. You might decide to use the cinematographic trick of 'jump cuts' and begin a new scene as though nothing happened in- between, allowing the reader to figure it out.

Quick descriptions

You might need a quick description of a place or person. The person may be relatively unimportant to the story. You could do a quick 'telling' sketch, making sure you do not give that person undue importance.

Show and Tell

I did not realise until a few years back, until I started seeing it in a manuscript, that it is possible to show *and* tell.

The author had the villain plan in meticulous detail with his underling about executing a particularly nefarious kidnapping. Since this had not actually happened at that time in the story, it was all 'tell.'

Later in the story, the minion executes the same plan, and the story was mostly 'shown'. The execution of the plan went like clockwork; it did not deviate even a bit from the plan.

'Ah,' I thought, unconsciously paraphrasing the Bard, 'the tedium of a twice-told tale.'

Chapter 2
Point of View

Rule 2: Mind Your POV

Point of View (POV) is the narrative voice that is telling the story. A narrative point of view is defined by:

- who is narrating
- whether the person narrating is a character in the story
- what the narrator knows about the characters

There are three principal points of view:

- first person
- third-person omniscient
- third-person limited

First- person POV

The person telling the story refers to herself as 'I'. Usually, she is a character in the story. When most people start, they write in the first person about their experiences. Even though it may seem the most natural thing to do, it has several limitations and pitfalls.

There are some advantages in using the first- person POV:

Easy to relate for the reader

A reader can instantaneously relate to a first-person narrative. The 'narrative distance' is small. By giving access to the emotions, thoughts, words, and actions of the first-person character, you draw the reader into the story.

Fewer unintentional errors of POV

In one sense, it is easier to write. You won't make unintentional errors of POV because when you write in first-person POV, you are in the space you normally inhabit in real life. The difficulties lie in dealing intimately with a first-person persona very different from you.

First person other than the protagonist

Using a first-person character other than the protagonist of the story provides a layer of indirection. This is useful in detective stories where the story is told through the eyes of a secondary character. Think Watson relating a Sherlock Holmes story.

Cons of first- person POV

Limited in style/tone

The narrative is limited by the character's knowledge and language. If the first-person character is substantially different from yourself (as a writer), it may be difficult to keep the correct tone throughout the entire story. For instance, if the first person is an adolescent or a psychopath or unlettered, it can get difficult (particularly if you are mature, balanced, or literate). The authorial voice usually cannot come to the fore. You have to write necessarily in the style of the first-person persona.

Limitation in plotting

Everything that is written has to be from the character's personal knowledge, inference, or hearsay. This limits the narration in many ways. If two things happen at the same time in different places, since the character cannot be at both places at once, the author will have to describe it from hearsay or not at all. This imposes a limitation on the plotting and may induce some forced 'telling'.

There could be too much exposition

All the emotions and reactions of the various characters are filtered through the first-person character. This can prove to be a blessing or a bane. Watch against a tendency for too much exposition.

Examples of first person

My father's family name being Pirrip, and my Christian name Philip, my infant tongue could make of both names nothing longer or more explicit than Pip.

CHARLES DICKENS, *GREAT EXPECTATIOINS*

When he was nearly thirteen, my brother Jem got his arm badly broken at the elbow. When it healed, and Jem's fears of never being able to play football were assuaged, he was seldom self-conscious about his injury.

HARPER LEE, *TO KILL A MOCKING BIRD*

Third omniscient POV

The narration is, well, omniscient—all-knowing. There is no single perspective but a broad one that encompasses all characters, a godlike understanding of the story world, including a knowledge of what is going to happen.

> Raj hoped that the aliens would go away, thinking the place deserted. Sam was hoping to meet them. He simply did not know what untold evil they could bring.

Pros of the omniscient POV

It is relatively easy to maintain.

Sometimes, through omniscient narration, an author can convey her philosophy and worldview rather than allowing the reader to draw his own conclusion. It can aid or defeat the author's objectives, depending on the context.

It is also much easier to foreshadow happenings, contributing to creative tension.

> Little did he know that this was going to prove to be extremely dangerous for him.

This kind of foreshadowing is a little outdated. You see fewer and fewer instances, even in omniscient writing.

You can also create a persona of a narrator who is distinct from the characters in the story and from yourself.

Mulliner, a character in the books of PG Wodehouse, is one such example.

Disadvantages of the omniscient POV

Since the author herself is a step away from the characters and what is happening in the narration:

- the reader will also be not that involved
- the author can get preachy without noticing it

If you don't write it properly, an omniscient account can lead to head-hopping and some serious confusion.

Examples in literature

Many fairy tales and novels, for instance, *Pride and Prejudice* by Jane Austen, are told in the third- person omniscient point of view.

Terry Pratchett uses flights of omniscient narration in his *Discworld* series. So does Douglas Adams in his *The Hitchhiker's Guide to the Galaxy: The Trilogy of Four*, often in footnotes.

The taller of the pair was chewing on a chicken leg and leaning on a sword that was only marginally shorter than the average man. If it wasn't for the air of wary intelligence about him, it might have been supposed that he was a barbarian from the Hubland wastes. His partner was much shorter and wrapped from head to toe in a brown cloak. Later, when he has occasion to move, it will be seen that he moves lightly, catlike.

TERRY PRATCHETT — *COLOUR OF LIGHT*

As you can see, the narrator not just knows what is happening, he even knows what is going to happen.

In fact, what he was really looking out for when he stared distractedly into the night sky was any kind of flying saucer at all. The reason he said green was that green was the traditional space livery of the Betelgeuse trading scouts.

Ford Prefect was desperate that any flying saucer at all would arrive soon because fifteen years was a long time to get stranded anywhere, particularly somewhere as mindbogglingly dull as the Earth.

DOUGLAS ADAMS, *HITCHHIKER'S GUIDE TO THE GALAXY*

The omniscient narration is clear in the passage quoted.

The Book Thief by Markus Zusak is written from a unique perspective—first-person omniscient. The story is told by Death!

Third-person limited POV

Imagine you are right by the side of the character. You see what the character sees, hear what he hears, smell what he smells and feel what he does. You also know his thoughts.

A lot of fiction is written this way. The third-person limited POV also promotes the idea of 'show, not tell' as the reader takes a journey with the POV character.

Pros of third person limited POV

You secure a greater identification and involvement from the reader when compared to the omniscient point of view.

It is easier to keep secrets from the reader. If the POV character does not know about something, the reader will not know it either. As an author, if you want to hide something from the reader (say, in a murder mystery), all you have to do is hide it from the POV character.

It is easier to control the narrative distance from the reader. The writing can range from knowing the innermost thoughts of the POV character to just following the action.

Unlike in the first person, it is easy to describe the physical appearance of a POV character. For instance, you cannot write:

> I am 5 feet 10 inches tall. I have blue eyes and pearly teeth, and an air of mystery about me.

At least, not without sounding awkward.

The third-person point of view allows you to shift between multiple perspectives and even identify the various POV characters by name, unlike the first person, which uses the ubiquitous 'I'. Unlike in the third person, in the first person, you need a device to tell who the POV character is, either by naming the chapter/scene with the name of the character, or by introducing oneself, or have someone call the character by name, etc.

Disadvantages of the third-person limited POV

It is more difficult to write in that you cannot delve into other minds at will. It is also easy for you to slip out of the point of view.

> Gopi trudged along the forest. His companion was tired and slowly started lagging.

If the lines given above are written from the POV of Gopi, he cannot know that his companion is tired. (To establish that you need body language or dialogue.)

Unintentional 'head-hopping' can occur as in:

He was certain what their goals were, but she was less certain.

Examples of third-person limited

> *Harry whiled away the hours until dawn in front of the fire, getting up now and then to stop Crookshanks sneaking up the boy's staircase again. At long last Harry thought it must be time for breakfast, so he headed through the portrait hole alone.*

JK Rowling, *The Prisoner of Azbakan*

Dima ignored Pyotr's smug look; he wiped his hands and put on his coat and hat. Mama handed him tin lantern. 'Hurry now,' she said, pushing up his collar to keep his neck warm. 'Scurry back and I'll tuck you in and tell you a story.'

'A new one?'

'Yes, and a good one, about the mermaids of the north.'

'Does it have magic in it?'

'Plenty. Go on, now.'

Dima cast his eyes once to the icon of Sankt Feliks on the wall by the door, candlelight flickering over his sorrowful face, his gaze full of sympathy, as if he knew just how cold it was outside.

LEIGH BARDUGO, *KING OF SCARS*

The majority of fiction is written in the third person.

Some flavours of third-person limited POV

Objective POV

Objective POV works like a camera in a movie. It is a view of a fly on the wall. It is more commonly used in non-fiction. In an objective point of view, the narrator does not have access to the thoughts and feelings of the characters.

Oliver took the plate and began to eat. The food was cold and hard, but Oliver was so hungry that he ate it all.

When he had finished, the master turned away again.

Oliver looked at the plate. There was still a little food left on it. He knew that if he asked for more, he would only make the master angrier.

But he was so hungry.

He looked at the food again. He looked at the master. He looked at the food again.

"Please, sir," he said. "I want some more."

If we were to rewrite the above from an objective POV:

Oliver took the plate and began to eat. He ate it all.

When he had finished, the master turned away again.

Oliver looked at the plate that still had a little food left on it.

He looked at the food again. He looked at the master. He looked at the food again.

"Please, sir," he said, "I want some more."

You should be able to make the reader feel the emotion by inferring it rather than hitting the reader over the head with emotionally charged passages or dialogue.

Deep POV

Deep POV is a kind of limited POV in which the narrative voice directly describes the thoughts, feelings, and experiences of the POV character.

An example will illustrate the difference between a deep POV and a normal limited third-person POV.

Third-person limited POV

He looked into the distance and wondered if they were there to meet him.

Third- person deep POV

He looked into the distance. Are they here to meet me?

Narrative distance and narrative style

In the following list, the points of view are ordered in terms of increasing narrative distance (from the reader):

- first person
- second person
- third person — deep
- third person — limited
- third person objective
- third person omniscient

The choice of tense is also important. Using the present tense allows the reader to feel the closest connection to the narrative.

Unreliable narration

A good example of an unreliable narrator is Pi Patel, the narrator of Yann Martel's *Life of Pi.* He tells a story of being adrift at sea and sharing his lifeboat with a zebra, orangutan, hyena, and tiger.

In J. M. Coetzee's *Disgrace*, we can see that the narrating professor, David Lurie, is sexually exploiting a young college student, even though he defends his action and believes he has done nothing wrong. Later on in the story, we see the underlying tension in that the professor is racist, even though he does not believe he is so.

Here is a story told in the first person and retold from a third-person limited point of view. This story was popular about 60 years ago.

It is in Mary Smith's first-person point of view.

It got chilly inside the train compartment. I pulled my scarf more tightly around my shoulders and chanced a look at the British soldier seated opposite to me. His eyes were on the obviously German ex-soldier next to him. Was there a look of sneering contempt? God, I didn't know Germans were allowed on our trains and I edged closer to Mom, who placed a reassuring hand on mine. Suddenly, everything grew dark. After a moment of confusion, I realised that this was the Lindsay tunnel, but the crescendo of the steam engine frightened me.

In the darkness, to my horror, I heard a wet smacking kiss, followed immediately by the sound of a slap.

As the train pulled out of the tunnel, I saw the look on Mother's face and the look of bewilderment on the German's face. I figured out what had happened in a trice. Thank God the German didn't try kissing me. My mother clearly knew how to handle herself.

Notice that she has no access to the thoughts or emotions of others. Her thoughts and emotions are, however, clear to the reader.

Let us hear the real story from a third-person limited point of view. The POV is that of the British soldier.

He was returning home. The war was over, but the hatred remained. When he saw the face of the German next to him, he remembered the face of the comrades who had not returned from their mission. His lips curled in revulsion. He looked at the watch and knew that the Lindsay tunnel was due any moment now.

The train entered the tunnel and darkness and a crescendo of noise filled the compartment.

Now is the time.

After the train came out of the tunnel, he noticed with satisfaction the look on the German's face. The marks on his cheeks were now turning red. He detected the look of contempt on the old lady's face as she looked at the German, and what he fancied was the look of pride as her gaze settled on her daughter.

He realised that the back of his left hand was still a little wet with his own kiss and wiped it surreptitiously. His right hand still hurt from the ferocious slap he had delivered to the German.

'It was worth it. This was for you, Ed,' as he remembered a dead comrade.

You can think of an omniscient version of this.

Chapter 3
Dialogue

Rule 3: Let the Dialogue Multitask

Realistic dialogue

I often hear advice exhorting writers to write dialogue realistically. However, there is an issue with this advice. If you write dialogue realistically, you will probably bore the reader stiff. Do not make the dialogue too clever either, unless the character is likely to use clever words.

Here is some hyper-realistic dialogue.

'Hey, Sanjay, what sup,' said Ravan.

'What sup,' replied Sanjay.

'Long time, no see.'

'Been busy. And you? All well?'

'All well, Sanjay.'

'And I haven't seen you since, you know, what? You were there.'

Eliminate such 'realistic' dialogue. Well-written dialogue is not realistic. It *simulates* realism and focuses on the author's objectives.

You need to craft a piece of dialogue in an efficient manner to further your objectives and that of the book.

Dialogue tags

The purpose of the dialogue tag is primarily to help the reader figure out who said something (and sometimes, to whom).

'I am hungry,' Bhim said.

'Bhim said' is the dialogue tag.

I prefer not to use speech tags other than 'said' or 'asked', except on rare occasions. If the text of the dialogue does not give the impression of shouting, propping it with the tag 'shouted' would appear artificial. The problem here is that the dialogue is weak.

Avoid as much as possible, words like 'explained', 'murmured', 'interrupted', 'remarked', 'observed', 'mentioned', 'uttered', 'vocalised', 'announced', 'averred', and 'avowed'. Stick to 'said', which is invisible and does not jar on repetition.

Although it is bad enough that you might want to use words other than 'said' or 'asked', this is not the worst you can do. Your characters may smile, laugh, chortle, and wink their words.

'I see you haven't shaved,' he smiled.

'That's rich,' she laughed.

I have tried 'smiling' my words. Let me assure you it is well-nigh impossible.

Avoid using adverbs in the speech tags whenever possible. If you want to 'susurrate rustlingly' or 'raspily' or 'chortle musically', can you please do it elsewhere? Readers get nauseated easily.

For one of my books, I had a publisher's editor from hell. She simply suggested alternative words for 'said' or 'asked' I had used within dialogue tags. I had to explain to her that 'said' and 'asked' in dialogue tags are practically invisible and often, it is better to stick to them. She relented only when I quoted Stephen King to her.

The last I saw her, she had a wistful look on her face, her eyes were blank, her hair disordered and she was murmuring something. I could catch only snatches of words.

'Expostulated wearily, shouted angrily, whispered urgently, murmured softly, exclaimed loudly….'

Let your speech tags primarily show who said something. Do not charge them with emotion, fit in the backstory, etc. into them. Do not write:

'D-d-don't go,' the grandmother, who had been abused as a child and hence developed a noticeable speech impediment, stammered.

Beats

A beat in a dialogue is an action that is performed by the speaker during, before, or after the dialogue. A beat may be:

- an action beat
- a reaction beat
- a tone beat

A reaction beat is used to show bodily and internal reactions not shown by the dialogue itself.

A tone beat emphasises the emotion behind the dialogue by describing the loudness, pitch, or speed of the words.

> 'Don't you dare take your hand out of my sight.' She spat out the words at a staccato clip.

Examples of beats

The following examples show the beat, 'he took a sip of the drink', before, during, and after the speech.

1. He took a sip of the drink. 'Nothing doing. I can never agree.' (Before)
2. 'Nothing doing.' He took a sip of the drink. 'I can never agree.' (During)
3. 'Nothing doing. I can never agree.' He took a sip of the drink. (After)

Note that the three methods above can imply different motivations. In Example 1, the sip of the drink may imply a little thinking before speaking. In Example 2, it might mean a certain deliberateness. In Example 3, it might indicate finality.

Some people advocate a specified number of beats in dialogue, for instance, three beats and a dialogue tag. Do what is appropriate; but whenever possible, use beats instead of tags while avoiding too many beats.

Add variety by changing beats to the beginning, middle, and end. Also, change the length of the tags and the type of beat.

Let there be movement beats. Even if the characters do not move a great distance away from their places, make sure that there is some physical movement. At the worst, let them twitch a bit. If two people sip tea and talk without moving for several pages, your reader will also want to take a tea break.

Objectives

The objectives for a piece of dialogue could be:

- moving the narrative along
- revealing character and dynamics in relationships
- reflecting the overall theme
- setting an appropriate mood for what follows
- revealing a bit of information to the reader without him believing

that the piece of dialogue exists for that purpose

- introducing or deepening a conflict

Ideally, it should serve more than one of the above purposes, with one out of the first four being mandatory.

Moving the narrative along

Dialogue can move the story along.

Do not use dialogue in an obvious manner for exposition or telling the backstory. The worst thing you can do in dialogue is for the characters to talk among themselves about things that they already know or ought to know, expressly for informing the reader. Avoid doing what I am about to do.

> 'Hey, how's your carpentry coming along, Muniyappa? Anyway, we know you are considered one of the most skilled wood-workers this side of the Indian Ocean, at least where we live, in Doddachikkanahalli, a small village in Karnataka, about 131 km. from Bangalore, along National Highway number 420.'
>
> 'I am fine, Basappa. Of course, you are continuing your work as a speech writer for the aspiring MLA for the Chikkadoddanahalli constituency. You told me yesterday that your son, Bangarukodukku, eighteen years old, studying in the twelfth standard, has run away from home. You also told me that the fifty-year-old Lalithamma, who teaches English in his school and had hopes of becoming the vice principal, has also been missing. Have they both returned home yet?'
>
> 'Why do you ask?' asked Muniyappa, B.A., who had started dyeing his hair a henna orange. 'I just told you this morning when I met you… Ah, I understand. They have not returned home. As I showed you this morning, my son has left behind a letter asking me not to search for him. The letter, as I told you, has corrections in red ink in a different hand, and a final remark, "can do better".'
>
> 'His mother, Lakshmamma, pushing fifty, must be unhappy as well at this turn of events, at least according to what you told me,' said Basappa, his wooden leg dragging on the asphalt road with a screeching noise.

'Very true, it is a grave story,' acknowledged Muniyappa.

'That reminds me,' said Basappa, 'I forgot what you did with the corpse. What did you do?'

Don't write thus.

Revealing character and dynamics of relationships

What people say reveals character. People could be long-winded, indirect, mono-syllabic, or imprecise in their speech, and all of this reveals character. What is said and even left unsaid shows the dynamics of the relationship between the speakers.

"Darling, I will be the happiest man on earth if you say 'yes' to me."

No reply.

"Will you marry me?"

Silence.

'I'll do anything for you. My life is in your hands. Why don't you say something? Anything. What's in your mind? Even if you say no, I'll accept quietly and steal away; away into the silence of the night, never to see you again. Never to be heard of again. Say something, please.'

'I thought you would never ask.'

Reflecting the theme

At least in one or two places in your book, let the dialogue reflect the theme of the book without making it blindingly obvious. However, if the theme, let us say, is revenge and you have nominated the protagonist to carry out the deed, don't have him quote Gandhi and say, 'An eye for an eye ends up making the world blind.'

If the dialogue that reflects the theme occurs early enough in the book, an astute reader will have a clue about the theme of your book and will be on the lookout for events that emphasise that theme.

A good dialogue is one that meets an objective. A great dialogue is one that achieves several things at the same time.

The following piece of dialogue occurs in *Slaughterhouse-Five,* early in the book and reveals the theme of war and death.

Over the years, people I've met have often asked me what I'm working on, and I've usually replied that the main thing was a book about Dresden.

I said that to Harrison Starr, the movie-maker, one time, and he raised his eyebrows and inquired, 'Is it an anti-war book?'

'Yes,' I said. 'I guess.'

'You know what I say to people when I hear they're writing anti-war books?'

'No. What do you say, Harrison Starr?'

"I say, 'Why don't you write an anti-glacier book instead?"

What he meant, of course, was that there would always be wars, that they were as easy to stop as glaciers. I believe that, too.

Introducing or deepening a conflict

Here is a passage from *The Princess Bride*.

'Welcome,' Vizzini called when the man in black was almost upon them.

The man in black stopped and surveyed the situation.

'You've beaten my Turk,' Vizzini said.

'It would seem so.'

'And now it is down to you. And it is down to me.'

'So that would seem too,' the man in black said, edging just a half-step closer to the hunchback's long knife.

With a smile, the hunchback pushed the knife harder against Buttercup's throat. It was about to bring blood. 'If you wish her dead, by all means keep moving,' Vizzini said.

The man in black froze.

'Better,' Vizzini nodded.

No sound now beneath the moonlight. ...

... 'Let me explain—' the man in black began, starting to edge forward.

'You're killing her!' the Sicilian screamed, shoving harder with the knife. A drop of blood appeared now at Buttercup's throat, red against white.

The man in black retreated. 'Let me explain,' he said again, but from a distance.

William Goldman, *The Princess Bride*

Notice how the tension is increased gradually.

Limitations

You have no control over some aspects of dialogue. Each character speaks the way she does, sometimes against your wishes. Well, you made your bed, and now you must learn to lie down on it.

You can neither have an uneducated person spout big words nor can you have the strong silent types deliver long monologues. You also cannot have Sherlock Holmes explaining his methods except at the denouement.

Structure of dialogue

Beginning, middle, and end

Like the story, a passage of dialogue should also have a beginning, middle, and end. Start the dialogue and scene as late as you can and end it as quickly as possible after the objective is served.

Reversals and an undercurrent of conflict make dialogue exciting.

The dialogue could start out as pleasant and end in a brawl, or one character can start out as pugnacious and by the end of the dialogue, become calm.

It could be a lover's tiff ending in a reconciliation.

Notice the reversal in the following snippet:

> 'Hey, how wonderful to see you. Fancy bumping into you,' said Stanley.
>
> 'Considering that you have been tracing my movements for the last one week — '
>
> 'Hey man, don't take that attitude.'
>
> 'If you don't stop following me, I'll knock your block off. You know, I was the middleweight boxing champion in college. What you are doing is illegal.'
>
> 'More illegal than stealing letters from a defenseless girl?'
>
> Robert had no answer. How did Stan know?

Subtext/layers

What is left unsaid is as important as what is said, and having an undercurrent of subtext makes the narrative richer. The subtext can layer the story in multiple ways. It can —

- add to the character
- add to the theme
- foreshadow
- deepen the mystery that will keep the reader's attention engaged

When one character relates to the subtext of what the other is saying, you create marvellous dialogue. It can even happen when one character completely misses the obvious subtext.

In the following piece, Jabala attempts to seduce the three-headed demon, Trisaras, into revealing the location of his life force. The reason her words and actions are over the top is that *rakshasas* (demons) are notoriously unsubtle.

Trisiras looked up at the sound of Jabala's anklets. He rubbed two of his eyes in apparent disbelief.

'Yes, I am the real one, my life-master,' she said.

Trisiras got up, stumbled and regained his balance.

'Did you just call me your life-master?' he asked.

'Yes, and I also meant to call you my piece of jaggery.'

'The love of my life, my very existence,' he said and caught her in a tight embrace and showered fiery kisses on her forehead, lips and chin, while another tongue snaked deep into her mouth. Or so he would have, if he had read The Fragrant Lawn — Or what the Gnomons don't teach you. He hadn't, so he didn't. Instead, he squirmed slightly.

'Do you really mean it?' he asked.

'Yes, I do. However, our love must remain unfulfilled...' Jabala paused a little and sighed deeply and audibly.

'Why? Is there someone else that you like? Tell me who it is and I will eat him up. Then, not only will that person be out of the way, I would also have gained the qualities you like by eating him.'

'No, no. It is because I am afraid. Very afraid.' Again, she wanted to pause but was worried that Trisiras would fill up the gap by saying something. She settled for a beat. 'I am afraid that what I love will end up dying. When I was young, I had a mayfly as a pet. I still remember the day

it died. Come to think of it, that was the day I found it and put it in a matchbox.'

'Don't worry. Stick with me and I will catch you two mayflies every day.'

'You mistake me. I am worried about you. True, you are big and strong and have a way with Ganda Beranda birds. What if you should...' She turned away from him, put an arm over her eyes and whispered with a realistic catch in her throat, '... die?'

D. KALYANARAMAN, *SORCERER OF MANDALA*

Agenda

Let each character have their separate agenda during the dialogue. The dialogue will then have an element of conflict.

Character quirks

Give character quirks and distinct manners of speaking to different characters, but don't overdo it. Don't be too liberal with 'limps', 'nervous tics', 'squint-eyes', 'flowing beards', and 'wooden legs'.

There can be all kinds of markers that could make a character unique.

It could be a tendency to repeat some empty filler words. I use that with one of my characters who loves to use 'you see' as a filler.

It could be sarcasm, biting wit, humour, clever talk, ungrammatical speech, or long words occasionally misused—you name it.

Dialogue and pacing

I have elaborated on this in a section titled 'Pacing' in Chapter 4.

Cultural idioms that can add spice

If you are writing about a non-English culture, literal translation of some sentences spices up the story. Take care you don't do it too often.

I looked at him, greatly puzzled. The man was talking as if he were moving to the next street.

R.K. NARAYAN, *THE ENGLISH TEACHER*

Here is a dialogue from Chinua Achebe's *Things Fall Apart*.

The crowd answered- 'Ee-e-e!'

'We are giving you our daughter today. She will be a good wife to you. She will bear you nine sons, like the mother of our town.'

'Ee-e-e!'

The oldest man in the camp of the visitors replied: 'It will be good for you and it will be good for us.'

'Ee-e-e!'

'This is not the first time my people have come to marry your daughter. My mother was one of you.'

'Ee-e-e!'

'And this will not be the last, because you understand us and we understand you. You are a great family.'

'Ee-e-e!'

'Prosperous men and great warriors.' He looked in the direction of Okonkwo. 'Your daughter will bear us sons like you.

'Ee-e-e!'

How to answer a question

In real life, people answer questions tangentially. No one answers the question 'why did you do this?' with 'I did this because…'

You can answer a question with another question. You can provide an entirely unexpected answer.

'Hey, how're you?'

'What made you invite my girlfriend for dinner?'

'I didn't. She did.'

The first person is disconcerted for a moment.

'So, if she invites you for form's sake, you accept, is it?'

'I didn't.'

'So, who did she go out for dinner with?'

Dialogue as a social marker

The accents of various speakers are often a marker for culture, race, and class. As much as possible, don't use accents in written speech. Charles Dickens may have done it, but now it is passé.

It is fine to be ungrammatical in speech, but don't do accents.

Appropriate to the time and space

Ensure that the language the characters speak is appropriate to the time and place depicted, especially when you are writing a historical piece. One such writer who had mastered the language of the period was Georgette Heyer. Of course, the regency period lasted less than a decade, but she beautifully captures the manners of speaking of the period.

> *'Yes, it's all very well to talk like that, my dear, but I'm sure it's natural she should want a bit of gaiety, even though her Aunt Burford didn't see fit to bring her out this year. What's more, my dear—and I don't scruple to own it, for well I know I can say what I choose to you, and no harm done!—if Tiffany was to find it too slow for her here there's no saying but what she'd beg her uncle to fetch her away, which he would do, because it's my belief he didn't like sending her back to me above half, and no wonder!'*
>
> GEORGETTE HEYER, *THE NONESUCH*

Chapter 4
Pacing

Rule 4: Control the Pacing

What is pacing?

Pacing is the apparent speed at which the narrative moves. The apparent speed is the instantaneous velocity and not the overall speed. We are discussing the passage of psychological time, not actual time.

Pacing keeps the reader engaged and keeps him turning the pages. This does not mean that all your writing must take the reader along at breakneck speed. While this may be appropriate for certain kinds of fiction, often, the reader needs a breather. You may have to slow down the pacing deliberately.

What determines pacing?

The following list is in order of increased pacing.

Narration:

- digressions, long sentences
- exposition
- extraneous descriptions
- interior thoughts and monologue
- the use of present tense that often increases the pace

Dialogue:

- dialogue tags with several beats
- dialogue

Action scene:

- with focus on the action
- short sentences with focus on action

Note that dialogues and action scenes with focus and short sentences increase the pacing.

Let me explain with examples, things that slow the pacing down. In the following examples, the protagonist, Arthur, confronts the antagonist, Bloodred. Let me remind you once more—do not write thus!

Digression

Bloodred threw the dagger at Arthur. Arthur could see that the dagger was very sharp. His horse was poised to break into a trot at a single command or even at a single glance. It was even beginning to do so at a single thought. The horse had been a constant companion since his days at the training academy. It had once cleared a stream 20 feet in width in a single leap. Encouraged by the negligent pat by Arthur, the horse had again jumped and had fallen into the water while Arthur struggled with the dagger stuck deep into his neck.

Exposition with backstory

Bloodred threw the dagger at Arthur. Arthur remembered the first time he met Bloodred. Both were six at that time. Bloodred had gorged at the school cafeteria, but also wanted Arthur's lunch, that his mother had packed, leaving no food for herself, her facial features racked with pain, her hands trembling with ague, her body stooped with malnourishment...

Extraneous descriptions

Knowing Bloodred, he knew that the dagger must have been coated carefully with some little-known poison, with no known antidote. He knew that the dagger must have been sharpened on both sides and the point also must have been meticulously sharpened. The horse also whinnied. He could detect a note of desperation in its whinny. His legs were encased in moccasins worked in gold. The saddle was comfortable, though ornate.

Long sentences

While neither Bloodred, who had established a reputation over the known universe as a villain of the most heinous hue, nor Arthur, who had a reputation that would not fill a small-sized thimble, could picture a world in which both of them existed—a world torn asunder by strife of good against evil, a world in which no one was safe until they had taken sides, and even then only for a short while, apparently Bloodred had the larger appetite, for he had drawn his dagger in a trice and thrown it unerringly at Arthur.

Interior monologue

Even as the dagger that Bloodred threw was in the air, Arthur had a thought. Perhaps I should duck. How fleeting life is. Here now, not here an instant later. Is Bloodred's intent reflected on the gleaming dagger that twisted as it came? Should I let go? How would Guinevere feel? Would she be relieved? Would she welcome the killer of her former paramour with open arms? Or will she feign a smile on her tired lips, eyes empty as the stomach of an Arthurian peasant and welcome him with equally empty words? Or will she take a dagger to him — not this one, of course.

Arthur did not duck.

Stuffed dialogue tags

'Ha,' said Bloodred, triumphantly unsheathing a short dagger that had been the cause of many a death in the known universe.

'Ha, ha,' chortled Arthur, not to be outdone by a mere demon in human clothing, scratch that, in some form of barbaric attire, pausing to scratch his nose.

'See this,' said Bloodred as he twirled the dagger around in such a way that it caught the sunlight, 'This is what you are going to experience,' he said this in gloatingly final words.

'I see,' said Arthur, adjusting his waist belt, 'your foolishness reflected truly on the dagger.' Do you think, 'he continued, after adjusting his abdomen guard, 'I am frightened? I am not,' he concluded, throwing out his chest, and throwing out his back.

'Shut up, both of you,' said a third voice sharply. 'Let me do the talking.' It was the dagger.

Short dialogues without attribution

Dialogues of short sentences without speaker attribution quicken the pace of the action. Here is a part of a scene from my book, *Songs of the Cauvery*.

Note how the dialogue quickens the pace of the narrative and increases the tension.

When they arrived at his makeshift office, Hall didn't get up from the chair or even look up.

'Your name?' asked Hall, in his accented Tamil.

'Ranjitham.'

'Father's name?'

Silence.

Hall looked up. Turned to Tulasi. 'Write, 'doesn't know'.'

'Mother?'

'Parvatam.'

'Occupation? Oh, don't bother, write 'prostitute'.'

'No, I am not a common prostitute. I am a devadasi dedicated to Lord Kumbeswara.'

'And you live at...'

'11, Attakkaran Street.'

'Who else lives there?'

'My mother, Varadu, a distant relative, a maid servant and myself.'

'Do you know a Panju, Pancha... Pancha...'

'Panchapakesan, Sir,' Chanduru intervenes.

They already know. Stick to the truth as much as possible. There will be a time for outright lying.

'Yes.'

'You meet him often?'

'He has come home a couple of times. He has come to some of my performances.'

'You are intimate with him?'

Silence.

'What does he do?'

'He is a Brahmin boy who was studying in Kumbakonam and now has a job.'

'Where?'

'Some press. I don't remember the name.'

'Where is he now?'

A beat. 'I haven't seen him for some time. I don't know.'

The point of entry

It is often better to start a scene *in medias res,* that is, beginning in the middle of things, just when the action is starting. This ensures the reader's engagement. In fact, a dialogue, a chapter, a book — you can start all of these right in the middle.

However, don't wait until too late. Don't start with something like:

> Before he left, he took one last look at the body as he wiped the bloodstains off his hand.

Conclusion

- You can increase the pacing with short sentences. You should, however, vary the length of the words to avoid monotony.
- Dialogue increases the pacing.
- Action scenes without interruption increase the pacing.
- Enter a scene or dialogue as late as possible.

Chapter 5
Scenes

Rule 5: Make a Scene

One way of writing a book is almost entirely through scenes. You take the reader on a journey on the shoulders of the POV character and then automatically promote showing over telling.

What is a scene?

Scenes are coherent continuous bits of chapters. They can even comprise the entire chapter. In a scene, you have the same characters, the same time period, and the same place. If any of it changes, you have a different scene. It is fine to have characters enter and exit the scene. It works when the microcosm of the scene reflects the macrocosm of the overall theme of the story.

Beginning, middle, and end

The beginning has a hook and may have words that transition from the previous scene.

The middle has actions that attempt to fulfil the desire implicit in the beginning. It often has twists, turns, and reversals.

The end has a resolution, either of fulfilling the desire or being foiled.

Beginning/hook

> I didn't remember shooting this guy. Besides, if I had shot him, it would have been a head shot. The body lay prone, and I used my boots to flip him over. Mordizh! He was lucky I hadn't seen him first. Lucky? Whatever.

Middle

> I searched the room. I was getting tired until I got to the left drawer on the ornate desk. Initially, I found nothing interesting. There was a box of striped condoms, a large sand timer, an assortment of

hairpins, and a wad of 100-dollar bills. On an instinct, I put my hand into the drawer. I realised that the drawer wasn't as long as it should be. I pulled out the compartment completely, spilling the contents. I reached into the opening. My hands brushed against a knob. There was a secret compartment. I pulled out the compartment.

It was a thick manila envelope sealed with the emblem of the Government of Modrovia.

End

I heard a noise from behind. The dead body was now sitting up and grinning at me.

"Fooled ya, didn't I," it said.

"You are better off dead," I said, even as I shot him, right between his close-set eyes.

I returned to the table to retrieve the envelope.

"Put your hands up," a fresh voice said.

Note the twists and reversals (dramatised and dialled-up in the sample to illustrate a point) and the transition to the next scene. When the end of a scene coincides with that of a chapter, consider ending with a hook to make the reader read on. You could also transition into the next chapter or end with a foreshadowing.

How to create a hook

One way to create a hook is by starting off with strong action or an event that induces powerful emotion. Another is by raising questions in the reader's mind regarding interesting events and statements in the text. You create questions like 'what', 'what next', 'why', 'how',' and 'where' in the reader's mind.

What?

The answer to the question 'what' can be weak and put off the reader.

The figure walked through the mists. It then disappeared behind the trees.

If you continue in this vein for a page or two, the question in the reader's mind will be not 'what is the mystery figure', but 'what kind of trashy story am I reading?' This can work with some other detail. For instance:

The figure walked through the mists, stooping once to pick up something shiny from the ground. It threw the object into the distance.

What next?

I never dreamt that I would get into a boxing ring with a kangaroo.

Why?

I have never been much of a reader. Now I had to read 1500 pages of closely written manuscript from an ancient book.

How?

This is how I wrestled a grizzly and married the girl I loved on the same day.

Where?

As it often happens here, there was a tremendous commotion in the bazaar.

Some of the examples given are overdramatic, to illustrate the points. You don't have to be so. However, go ahead, if you can write timeless prose like:

'It was the best of times; it was the worst of times.'

CHARLES DICKENS, *A TALE OF TWO CITIES*

Or, *It was a pleasure to burn.*

RAY BRADBURY, *FAHRENHEIT 451*

The power of anticipation

You just have to stimulate the curiosity of the reader to ensure that he keeps reading. In fact, even more powerful than asking a question is to state the fact and let the reader anticipate.

For instance, *Songs of the Cauvery* starts with:

If she were older than thirteen, or had someone with whom she could have shared her problems, Mangalam wouldn't have decided to kill herself.

The anticipation carries the reader through the entire scene— that is imbued with a surreal hue — even though the reader knows exactly what is likely to happen. This is an example of a possible negative outcome. The curiosity of the reader can be piqued equally through a declared positive outcome.

I believe this kind of foreknowledge lurks in a corner of the reader's mind, acting subliminally until it springs forth at the moment when the event happens, providing either a cathartic relief from grief or a frisson of pleasure at the delayed gratification.

When to enter the scene?

Don't follow the King's advice to Alice:

> *"Begin at the beginning," the King said, gravely, "and go on till you come to the end: then stop."*
>
> LEWIS CARROLL, ALICE IN WONDERLAND

Rather, like a lover well-schooled in foreplay yet inexpert, enter late and leave early.

Start the scene as late as possible, *in medias res,* and don't stick around for the resolution.

For instance, don't start with a long description of the friendship between Anita and Priya and the reasons they had a dispute. Instead, get into an action scene.

Perhaps start with:

The blow to the face made Anita reel.

Don't end with details like what kind of plaster she used to dress her wound (unless, of course, the plaster had been doused beforehand with a little-known botulism-causing toxin).

Objectives of a scene

A scene needs to fulfil a function. It should:

- move the story forward
- reveal/reiterate/develop character
- deepen the theme
- set the mood
- introduce/deepen/resolve a conflict

The scene should do more than one of the above. Let us examine this in further detail.

Move the story forward

The story moves forward by the unfolding of the plot through:

- action
- dialogue
- inner thoughts and monologue

At times, give the main character and the reader a bit of respite from all those shootings, mortal wounds, gore, and miseries galore. Put her/him in a safe space and allow one and all, including the reader, to breathe in an interlude.

Develop character

The scene could introduce a new aspect of the protagonist's character or reiterate through an event that could even have happened in the past. The main character may also develop new insights and learning. Make sure that the characters 'remain in character' through the scene.

Once in a while, make sure that they act in ways that are even contrary to their instincts. A hero who is entirely goody-goody and not flawed even a little is uninteresting (not to say unrealistic) and a villain who is the personification of all evil is a cardboard cutout.

You might want your villain to fondle his favourite cat with one hand while strangling the life out of a childhood friend with the other.

Deepen the theme

An echo of the theme in a scene always helps but in moderation. Don't beat the theme to death in every scene. You could introduce an event encapsulating the theme in a quick sketch, right at the beginning of your story.

Set the mood and more with imagery

The mood to be set has to reinforce the action in the scene.

> *Consoled by these visions, Smiley arrived at the King's Road, where he paused on the pavement as if waiting to cross. To either side, festive boutiques. Before him, his own Bywater Street, a cul-de-sac exactly 117 of his own paces long. When he had first come to live here, these Georgian cottages had a modest, down-at-heel charm, with young couples making do on fifteen pounds a week and a tax-free lodger hidden in the basement. Now steel screens protected their lower windows, and for each house three cars jammed the curb. From long habit, Smiley passed these in review,*

checking which were familiar, which were not; of the unfamiliar, which had aerials and extra mirrors, which were the closed vans that watchers like. Partly he did this as a test of memory to preserve his mind from the atrophy of retirement, just as on other days he learnt the names of the shops along his bus route to the British Museum; just as he knew how many stairs there were to each flight of his own house and which way each of the twelve doors opened.

JOHN LE CARRÉ, *TINKER TAILOR SOLDIER SPY,*

Notice the way le Carré combines the setting with Smiley's character to set a mood.

Jatin moved off the road and entered what seemed to be a thicket of trees, and Panju followed. A few minutes later, the sight that greeted him made him gasp. It was quite dark; but moonlight revealed a temple that lay nestled in a clearing among a thick clump of trees. On closer look, the cluster of trees resolved into a single banyan tree. The temple itself was in ruins; but a pillared pavilion made of granite stood intact in front. As Panju and Jatin walked towards the open pavilion, clouds obscured the moon and everything was dark except for a dull glow from inside the pavilion. They had to slow down to watch their steps.

The glow came from a single oil lamp atop an improvised wooden altar covered with a tablecloth. A framed picture of Kali, smeared generously with red ochre, was propped upright with some books. The edge of a long sword gleamed in the light of the lamp. The smell of sandalwood incense permeated the pavilion. It had started raining and there was the constant murmur of raindrops falling on leaves. The flame of the lamp, protected on three sides with makeshift partitions, held steady despite the wind. Three men stood in an attitude of reverence, casting long shadows behind them. Panju thought that he recognized one of them; but wasn't sure.

KALYANARAMAN DURGADAS, *SONGS OF THE CAUVERY*

Notice the mood created for the beacon of light in the form of the revolution during the dark days of the British rule.

When you describe the setting, make sure that you are focusing not on every single detail but only on the telling detail.

Sometimes, you can create the mood through something unreal—like in a dream sequence. The narrative works when it carries out the primary function of revealing the inner state—conflicts, fears, and anxieties in the dreamer's mind.

Conflict

Besides being essential for a story, a conflict adds to a scene. Conflict provides the obstacles to a character achieving her goals. This can originate even from within due to the character's psychological state. You can show conflict through plot changes, narration, actions, dialogue, thoughts of the character, and interior monologue.

Showing conflict through plot changes

One sure way to increase conflict in a scene is to ramp up the stakes—for the protagonist or the antagonist. Another is to pile up obstacles in the protagonist's way. Here is a trope I have read more than once. I don't remember, but I think I read it in a penny dreadful. The protagonist, Morgan, is in a cellar, bound, ruing his fate, thinking, 'What can be worse?' Then the cellar fills up with water and the water comes up to his chest level...

At this stage, as an author, what do you do? Do you have the hero break out of his shackles? No. Here is what you do. You bung in a deadly water snake or two and maybe add a few sharp stakes (no pun intended) coming out of the walls. You get the idea, don't you?

You can also raise the stakes for the antagonist or for the entire world, or even for the universe, if you are feeling particularly nasty.

The conflict can be a tough decision that needs to be taken.

Showing conflict through actions

The conflict can be physical, as in a fist fight, or can be a war of words. It can be subtle. A lift of an eyebrow, a pulse beating at the temple, or a whitening of knuckles can be more effective than a detailed description of emotions.

Conflict through dialogue

It is easy to reveal conflict through dialogue. You need to ensure that each person taking part in the dialogue has their own agenda.

The conflict would then emerge. You can also show conflict with subtext. You can use interior monologues effectively to bring out conflict.

See the section on dialogue for details and further examples. We looked at different ways you can portray the aim of a scene. The scene should multitask and meet several objectives at one go.

Constructing the scene

You may be a plotter who plots out chapters diligently along with a detailed outline before starting to write the story. Or you may be a pantser who prefers to write from the seat of your pants (make up as you go along). I strongly recommend that while constructing a scene, you become a plot fiend. Here is the rough sequence of the steps.

Answer the following questions on paper or on a computer file:

- What kind of a scene is it going to be?
- How will the plot advance in this? What is to be covered?
- What is the setting? How will it create the mood to enhance the objective of the scene?
- Who are the characters in this scene?
- Whose POV is it going to be?
- Do I need to transition the previous scene/chapter into the current one?
- How will the scene start? What will be the hook?
- Will there be dramatic reversals? Will there be a change in the characters' attitude towards themselves or other characters or towards life as experienced in the story?
- Will there be surprises in the scene for the reader, the main character, or the other characters? (Sometimes, even for the author!)
- Does the scene reveal some new conflict or deepen an existing one?
- What will happen at the end of the scene? (What do I work towards?)
- How do I end it? Is there going to be some foreshadowing?
- Do I need to transition to the next scene?
- Now outline the entire scene in your mind. See it happening in your imagination.
- Outline it on paper.
- Start writing.

Scenes in non-fiction

You might think scenes have a part to play only in fiction. Think again. Using scenes is an effective way of connecting with the reader and placing him in your world. A lot of what has been said in this chapter is, therefore, applicable to non-fiction as well.

Imagine you are writing a story on Bangalore's traffic problem. Start with an individual with whom the reader can connect.

> Nitin stared at the rush of cars and scooters in front. The traffic hadn't moved for the last ten minutes. He tried very hard not to imagine the disappointment on his seven-year-old daughter's face when he failed to show up for the annual day function. Not when she had been cast as the tooth fairy in the play. His mobile rang. It was his wife.

You could then go on to the problems faced by commuters. If you wish to show statistics of the number of new vehicles licensed in Bangalore, you could do it after you have established a connect with the reader.

Science writing

> *There is the obligatory blackboard, taking up most of one wall of his office. It doesn't take long for Hardy to spring up and start chalking it up with diagrams and equations—something that most of the quantum physicists I meet seem inclined to do.*
>
> *We start talking about some esoteric aspect of quantum physics, when he stops and says, "I started off the wrong way." To reset our discussion, he says, "Imagine you have a factory and they make bombs." He has my attention.*
>
> Anil Anathaswamy, *Through Two Doors at Once: The Elegant Experiment That Captures the Enigma of Our Quantum Reality*

Feminist writing

> *She came whizzing down the stairs, thrown like a dart. She was stark naked. Her hair had been chopped off, her head was turned back to front, she was missing some toes, and she'd been tattooed all over her body with purple ink, in a scrollwork design. She hit the potted azalea, trembled there for a moment like a botched angel, and fell.*
>
> *He said, "I guess we're safe."*
>
> Margaret Atwood, The Female Body

Life and death

Here is how Venki Ramakrishnan, winner of the Nobel Prize for Chemistry in 2009, starts a chapter in *Why We Die.*

> *In springtime, my wife and I will often take a walk in Hardwick Wood near Cambridge to see the riot of bluebells that cover the forest ground. Once, we were walking along a path when we came across ...*

Historical

> *While royal birthdays were always occasions for great festivities, this one was especially significant, as Sethu Lakshmi Bayi had turned ten years old. An exciting thrill descended upon the capital, for in Travancore custom decreed that princesses must wed before the age of eleven...*
>
> MANU PILLAI, *THE IVORY THRONE:* CHRONICLES OF THE HOUSE OF *TRAVANCORE*

Conclusion

The key idea in writing a scene is to bring the scene before the reader's eyes (while leaving enough for the reader's imagination), ensuring immersion and engagement.

PART 2: PARAGRAPHS

Chapter 6
Bad Paragraphs

Rule 6: Structure Your Narrative

A paragraph is a fundamental unit of a longer piece of writing. It is a set of sentences, kept together through a unifying single idea. The beginning and end of a paragraph serve as boundaries or transitions between two ideas. At the end of a scene or chapter, they serve as continuing incentives for the reader to read on.

The next time you read a book, read carefully the last paragraph that ends a chapter. You will understand what I mean.

Have a separate paragraph for the dialogue of each person.

When you write, make sure that the tense, mood, POV, style, chronology, voice, and tone are consistent.

Inconsistencies of tense

Do not change tenses within the same sentence. You may change tenses within a paragraph only if the time at which the events happen calls for it.

Switching tenses in a single paragraph

In general, don't switch tenses. Here is an example of a rare case where switching is needed.

> The book, *Songs of the Cauvery,* describes a period of transition between centuries. The British hadn't left India. Food shortages were the norm.

In the passage above, I have used three different tenses—'describes' is in the simple present, 'hadn't left' is in the past perfect and 'were' is in the simple past.

Switching tenses in a single sentence

Occasionally, you cannot avoid this, as in:

> I yawn. Even though I had walked for miles, I think I wasn't tired.

Please note that the main narration is in the present tense.

Switching tenses through a book

Avoid switching tenses through the book. However, there could be some exceptions to this.

Dream sequences

You can write dream sequences in the present tense, even if the book is in the third-person past tense.

To increase the tempo of the action

Using the present tense lends a certain immediacy and urgency to the narrative. For instance, even though I have written *Songs of the Cauvery* in the past tense, the climactic scene is in the present.

Quoting an author

A quote from a book or movie is always in the present tense.

> JK Rowling examines the magical life of a young wizard, Harry Potter, in *Harry Potter and the Philosopher's Stone*.

Using past perfect

When you are writing the backstory in the novel, you need to use the past perfect tense to refer to an action that happened before the time of the flashback. An example should clarify this:

> I had come to meet Ganesh. Ravi had accompanied me. I had walked while he had taken a taxi.

In the above sentences, the repeated use of 'had' can grate on the reader's nerves. You could instead write:

> (Recast) I had come to meet Ganesh. Ravi accompanied me. I walked while Ravi took a taxi.

You can also switch to the simple past tense after just one sentence.

The switching of tense in the following sentence is plainly wrong:

> (Wrong) He switched off the engine, got down, and a car runs over him.
>
> (Corrected) He switched off the engine, got down, and a car ran over him.

Inconsistent POV

Don't switch POV in the middle of a scene and definitely not within a paragraph.

First- person POV

When you are in the first- person POV (I, me, my, we, our), it is difficult to switch POVs. This is a good thing. Once in a while, you might write something on these lines:

> I stared at him. He didn't know why I was staring at him.

This is an obvious violation of the POV. You cannot know what is going on in the mind of others unless you are a mind-reading slugworm from Ganymede. To avoid this, you could infer emotion or thought from body language. For instance:

> I stared at him. I saw his blank stare. The lines on his forehead deepened. I knew then that he did not know why I was staring at him.

Third- person POV

It is far easier to make mistakes of POV in the third person. While it is ideal that you strictly adhere to the POV, for reasons of brevity, you might sneak in something that violates POV. This is called authorial license, also known as you-are-not-guilty-if-you-aren't-indicted.

Here is an example of some POV errors in the third person.

> The hunter blocked a thrust from the thug in front. The one behind her raised her cudgel to strike a blow.

The POV is that of the hunter and since she does not have eyes at the back of her head, she could not have known about the person behind her preparing to strike a blow.

You cannot know the thoughts, intentions, motivations, and emotions of others. What you see is what you get.

For a detailed treatment of POV, refer to the chapter on POV.

Inconsistent tone/style

Be consistent in tone, within a scene, and at the very least, within a paragraph. Do not switch from an informal tone to a formal one.

> You dudes must think what I have written is cool. But there is a caveat, a caveat so puissant and impregnated with meaning that, as Kant said — self-incurred is this tutelage when its cause lies not in lack of reason but in lack of resolution and courage to use it without direction from another. Sapere aude! 'Have courage to use your own

> reason!' — that is the motto of enlightenment. Way to live it up, guys! This is not acceptable.

> I got up as usual at 6 AM. I had a lot of work that I had brought home. I finished my shower. The morning air had a nip to it. I must wear a coat. I was involved in making the presentation. I had to get a particular toy my son had asked for. I wanted to animate parts of the presentation but I wasn't sure how to do it.

Can you see the incoherent chronology and order of ideas in the above passage? Within a paragraph, you must stick to a particular idea and also write in the order in which the micro-events happen.

Incoherent in general

> Man is a social animal. I am not sure if it is inevitable that all forms of governance will become democratic. We certainly don't exist in a vacuum. No man is an island. Autocracies are also not inevitable. Just to go abroad, I have to get a visa. I have to ensure my passport is up-to-date.

The paragraph given above does not make much sense, does it? Perhaps this is an extreme example. It exemplifies the need to have a coherent thread of thought running through your narrative.

Consider ordering your narrative chronologically or by idea, with a transition from one to the other or arranged along a storyline.

Back and forth

In a single block of text, say, in a chapter, do not switch back and forth between the formal and the informal, the general and the particular, the past and the present, and zooming in and zooming out. Let one segue into the other and also maintain an appropriate tone.

Multiple voices

It is not that multiple voices cannot be used at all. In *Songs of the Cauvery*, I have employed three different voices/tones — one, a lyrical voice while talking about the Cauvery and the metaphor she represents; a second slightly academic voice of a historian, used to narrate incidents of historical interest; and the third-person limited voice of the main story.

Unfulfilled promises

Do not set up any expectations that you cannot meet or make any promises you cannot keep, merely because it looks good in a paragraph. For instance, do not foreshadow something and not fulfil the implied promise of that foreshadowing. If you end a chapter or a scene with a hook, make sure it is not just a trivial one designed only to keep the reader engaged.

> Little did he know what was in store for him the moment he turned the corner.

Don't do this unless something drastic happens to the character at the corner. In fact, do not do it even then.

Transitions

- Observe the unity of time, place, participants, and ideas. When any of them changes, at the very least, include a paragraph break and transition into the next paragraph. Some major changes might need a scene break or even a chapter break.
- Some key transition words are: further, in addition, also, moreover, first (ly), second (ly), third (ly), last, and finally. Some other transition words are listed in Appendix 1.

One idea should be linked to the other. Transition words are necessary if the logic of what follows is clear in the writing. A transition sentence may be necessary to allow the paragraph to meld into the next. Do that only when necessary. Particularly in fiction, it should be fine to use jump cuts.

In non-fiction, you could use sub-heads without transition sentences.

Boring Paragraphs

You should keep the reader interested. Every paragraph must do one of the following:

- advance the topic/narrative/plot directly
- transition quickly to the next paragraph
- reveal character
- reinforce mood
- strengthen the theme

The last three are relevant mainly to fiction.

Ideally, the content should serve multiple purposes and fulfil more than one of the previous requirements. You have an unsaid covenant with the reader. In return for him spending time with your book, you agree to entertain, inform, or enlighten him in the best possible manner. You will break this covenant if you resort to circumlocution or equivocation.

Circumlocution

Circumlocution is the use of many words where a few would do, not approaching the topic directly, primarily in order to be evasive.

If a character indulges in circumlocution, it may be fine, either because it reflects the real world or because it reveals character. However, circumlocution is almost always bad if the author practises it in her narrative.

PG Wodehouse luxuriates in it purely for comic effect, as in:

> *He was staring before him with a smile so fixed and pebble-beached that I should have thought that anybody could have guessed that there sat one in whom the old familiar juice was splashing up against the back of the front teeth.*
>
> PG WODEHOUSE, *RIGHT HO, JEEVES.*

(Long-winded) I am planning to visit the hospital to see a medical doctor in order to effect a cure for my medical condition.

(Revised) I am seeing a doctor.

Use of scare quotes

Scare quotes are used to draw attention to an unusual or wrong use of a term.

There is no hard evidence of 'global warming'.

The author uses some terms reluctantly (knowing fully well that they are inadequate to convey the intended meaning). In other words, she is saying, 'I am smarter than that. Some idiot used these ridiculous words. You, the reader, are also used to such stupid terms. Would I use words like these if there were better options?'

Avoid scare quotes.

Self-indulgent writing

Even if you write for yourself, you have to take care to see that you write things that *you* would enjoy reading. Long philosophical ramblings that do not connect with the story, excessive amounts of detail in the setting, obscure cultural and literary references, private jokes — all come under this form of writing. You might let some of these darlings live in your first draft, but typically, these are the ones to be executed with extreme prejudice.

Complex paragraphs

A paragraph may be complex because of its content or form. If a complex idea needs to be conveyed, you can communicate it in a way that is easy to understand by either using simple language or by using a metaphor or simile.

The form of the paragraph is something that you can definitely control. Some factors that contribute to the complexity of the paragraph are length of the paragraph, use of unfamiliar and complex words, and use of jargon. The more complex the idea, the simpler should be the words describing it.

How long should a paragraph be?

The paragraph should not be so long that the reader's eyes glaze over. The end of a paragraph also provides some relief to the reader's eye with white space.

The paragraph can even be so short that it has only one sentence or one word.

In Kurt Vonnegut's book, *Slaughterhouse-Five,* there is a masterful paragraph with just one word:

Listen.

Another paragraph consists of just two words:

He says.

Structure

Like a scene, chapter, or book, the paragraph also has a beginning, middle, and end. This does not mean that you need at least three sentences to make up a paragraph. One sentence can convey the entire idea. For a long paragraph with a complex idea, the paragraph may have an introduction as the beginning, explanation in the middle, and a conclusion and preparation for the next paragraph as the end.

Dialogue as a separate paragraph

The normal convention is to have a separate paragraph for each piece of dialogue. It is a matter of stylistic choice whether you want to include the dialogue as a part of the paragraph or not. I suggest you do so only if you want that part of the narration to be a 'tell' and not a 'show'. Writers often use this in literary novels.

> I argued a lot with my father. 'I really don't like to see you cry,' he would say, brandishing a belt. I would stare sullenly. 'It pains me more than you,' he would say, once he had finished.

Compare this with:

> My father didn't like me arguing.
>
> 'I really don't like to see you cry,' he said, brandishing the belt again.
>
> I stiffened my back for the next blow.
>
> There was more than one.
>
> 'It pains me more than you,' he said.

You can see that both passages have different kinds of feel.

Insulting intelligence

Assume that you are writing for a careful and intelligent reader.

Careful reader

Writing for a careful reader means you do not repeat or even emphasise what you said, wrongly assuming that you will lose your point if you do not elaborate upon it.

It also means that you write with care. If you have written something that you have not researched or fact-checked properly, eventually, some reader is bound to bring it up. Worse, you will never know how many readers stopped reading your book because of that and how many actively told others not to read it.

Intelligent reader

It is better to let the reader infer from what you have written. You just have to place the dots and the reader will connect them for you. Do not rob the reader of this joy.

Talking down

One of the worst things you can do is to talk down to the reader. If you want to be preachy, pompous, or patronising, you will be talking to empty halls.

> *Again, when a righteous man doth turn from his righteousness, and commit iniquity, and I lay a stumbling-block before him, he shall die: because thou hast not given him warning, he shall die in his sin, and his righteousness which he hath done shall not be remembered; but his blood will I require at thine hand.*
>
> EZEKIEL 3.16: *KING JAMES VERSION* OF THE BIBLE

Warnings like these might have worked for some prophets of yore, but I would advise you strongly against taking such a tone now.

Indianisms

Good language is not an absolute that follows static rules. Much depends upon usage. What was considered wrong years ago by language purists may be perfectly fine today.

Language can vary from region to region. Still, if you want your writing to be appreciated universally, there are certain usages that are best avoided, at least till they become mainstream. I have discussed some usages peculiar to India in this section.

Some eccentricities in Indian English

Some words and phrases have made it into the written form of Indian English while some have remained only in speech. A few examples have been listed below:

Good name

Do not say or write, 'my good name is ....' You do not have two names, one good and one bad. 'My name is ...' will suffice.

Only

'Only' is an insidious word that takes on different meanings in different parts of a sentence.

Marlene had ice cream with noodles.

The meaning gets changed with adding 'only' in various positions in the sentence. We Indians think of even more positions to insert 'only'.

I am doing this now only. (I have just begun doing this.)

I am doing this for you only. (I am doing this specially for you.)

Avoid such usages till they become mainstream.

Pass out
'To pass out' is to faint. Using it to mean 'graduate' creates an avoidable confusion.

> I passed out in 1998.
> (I must have revived soon after.)

Prepone
This is a word that is not in normal usage. However, both the Oxford and the Cambridge dictionaries list it as a legitimate word.

If you can postpone things, why can you not prepone them? This is something that definitely needs to be a part of normal usage. In fact, it originally meant 'place in front of'.

Cope up
We Indians cannot 'cope' with things easily. We need to 'cope up' with them, but let us resist the temptation.

Kindly revert back
No, there is no need to regress to your childhood or even a previous life. 'Please reply' will do nicely.

Discuss about
Yes, we are guilty of this. We rarely 'discuss' things. We 'discuss about' them.

Take an exam
We like to 'take' exams rather than 'giving' them.

Do the needful
This is a relict from colonial times. Let us stop using this phrase.

Where are you put up?
It sounds as though someone erected a tent for me to live in. Perhaps that is the origin of the phrasal verb that means 'live'.

He said me to come
This is plainly wrong. 'He asked/told me to come' is fine.

I am having a lot of work
I am unable to trace the origins of using the present continuous at the drop of a turban. Just say 'I am busy' or 'I have a lot of work.'

I couldn't able to do it
(Corrected) I wasn't able to do it.

Out of station
Just say you are 'not in town'. You are no longer a government official in the colonial times, travelling on work.

Cousin brother/real brother
Unfortunately, English, in its present state of development, does not have distinct names for various relatives. Until it does, make do with 'cousin'.

Eat my head
This is a literal translation of an idiom in some Indian languages and does not work in English. It does not mean 'to nag' in English.

Please adjust
You can adjust a monkey wrench, your belt, etc., but this cannot be used to ask someone to be 'accommodative'.

Off the lights, off the on switch
I love this, but, well, this is not considered proper English. At least, not as yet.

Order for
Just 'order' things; don't 'order for' things.

Do one thing
'Do something'. You can dole out advice on what to do even without using this phrase.

Organise
Don't 'organise' mundane things, like getting someone some tea.

Dying to eat
This is a true story. A friend of mine politely refused biscuits when offered. The host took them away, muttering under her breath, 'OK, she is dying to eat biscuits' a literal translation of an idiom in Kannada, meaning — 'she would rather die than eat biscuits.'

She thus said the opposite of what she wanted to convey.

A poem in Indian English

Come Home

Myself Kalyan.
I am giving English grammar workshop.
What's your good name, sir?
My missus is out of door
So I am only the cooker
But my house you must definitely come.
Bring one bottle.
Foreign whiskey only.
Eversilver tumbler ok for you, no?
Ice also I will only provide
I'll cook you hot, hot pakoras.
Chips also I can buy.
You don't know where my house comes?
Go just straight straight on main road,
And turn right.
You can see my backside.
If you not coming,
kindly revert soon.
Don't forget bottle.

Outdated formalisms

Shun outdated formalities, such as:

- please be informed that
- be advised that
- shall revert to you
- in my humble opinion.

Babu English

While not too many people use the full formality, obsequiousness, and deviousness of *Babu* English, a gift from our colonial past, it is worthwhile to avoid even shades of it appearing in your writings.

Some examples of *Babu* English:

Respected Sir,

... It is with deep regret and unfeigned sorrowfulness that your poor slave approaches his poor tale at the footsteps of your honour's throne...

... Your most obedient, humble servant.

Being in much need and suffering many privations, I have after long time come to the determination to trouble your bounteous goodness. To my sorrow I have not the good friendships with many people, hence my slow rate of progress and destitute state. Here on earth who have I but thee, and there is Our Father in heaven, needless to say that unless your milk of human kindness is showered on my sad state no other hope is left in this world.[1]

Word order confusion

English is a right-branching language, whereas most Indian languages are left- branching. The order of subject followed by verb and then by object is not the norm in Indic languages. They have subject-object-verb as the normal order.

More problematic, particularly for Indians, is the word order used in English for clauses.

Adjective clauses and adverb clauses follow the respective noun or verb that they modify (unlike simple adjectives and adverbs that precede the modified word).

Let us consider a few examples:

The man, who has a crooked nose, lives nearby.

Indians tend to put the adjectival and the adverbial clauses first.

He has a crooked nose, no? That man lives nearby.

By sunset tomorrow, I will come to your house.

This makes the writing awkward.

Rule 6 needs to be discussed in more detail, but we will do it in the chapter on Structures and Patterns.

---

1 http://marymoore2012.weebly.com/blog/ english-as-a-global-language-babu-english

PART 3:
PHRASES/SENTENCES

Chapter 7
Incorrect Usage

Rule 7: Watch Your Grammar

Subject-verb agreement

Usually, the verb form used is singular if the subject is singular and plural if the subject is plural.

Examples of normal usage:

The King eats alone.

The courtiers eat in a group.

In this section, I have highlighted a few cases where the number to be used is not immediately obvious.

Collective nouns

Collective nouns refer to a group of animals (I include people here) or things taken as a whole. Examples include herd, committee, and bunch.

Always plural

Some collective nouns are always in the plural. Examples include mob, glasses, pants, trousers, and police (as a collective noun).

Where are my glasses?

Where are the police when you need them?

Always singular

Some collective nouns are always in the singular. Examples include everyone, everybody, no one, and nobody.

Everyone understands what I am saying.

Nobody loves me.

Context-dependent

Other collective nouns are singular when they behave as a group and plural when the action applies to individual members of the group, as in:

The herd is grazing peacefully. (Singular)

When a roar is heard, the herd bolt in different directions. (Plural)

Based on version of language

Most other collective nouns are treated as singular in American English and plural in British English. An example of the same is the word 'family'.

A group of items

Twenty items lay on his desk.

Twenty items is a bit too much, if you ask me.

In the first example, the items are considered individually and hence, as a whole, they are reckoned to be in the plural form. In the second example, a 'group of twenty items' is singular.

The only sight that greeted her eyes, amidst all the animals, was the embarrassment of pandas nibbling at a plywood sheet.

The way to lose weight is fewer ice-creams and more salads.

The above are correct sentences. Do not be misled by the proximity of the verb to a plural or collective noun.

Singular and plural uses of 'any, all'

All

All were registered for the workshop. ('All' is used as plural here and refers to many people, each of whom was individually registered for the workshop.)

All I want is a room somewhere. ('All' is used as singular here to denote 'the only thing'.)

All they saw was utter confusion. (The noun 'confusion' is used as singular and does not take a plural form as it is not countable.)

Any

Does any of us know correct English? (As singular)

Are any of my sentences right? (As plural)

Singular nouns that go together

Nouns that go together and are joined by 'and' can be considered a single unit and take the singular verb form. 'Rack and ruin' or 'bread and butter' are examples of such apposite nouns.

The rack and ruin of the place is assured.

The bread and butter of my business is words.

The fish and chips served by the restaurant was superb.

The verb referring to nouns that are joined by 'or' takes the number of the closest noun.

Only Blumenthal or I know it. ('know' is matched with 'I')

Either Ramu or Kishore is guilty.

Neither Kenilworth nor the beach boys know it.

Collective nouns, fractions

Collective nouns and fractions are in the singular.

The flock of geese swoops gracefully.

A keening of Yalis descends on them.

One half of hundred is fifty.

Number based on context

Each

Each of us is a writer.

We each are committed to writing.

The first example treats writers as a group and, therefore, in the singular. In the second example, the members of the group are alluded to separately and hence, in the plural.

None of

None of the spread remains uneaten. (The spread is treated as an undifferentiated mass and, therefore, in the singular.)

None of the writers have written about trivial things.

Treat 'none' as singular when it is used in the sense of 'not one' and plural when in the sense of 'not any'.

Not only... but also

Not only the books, but also your lifestyle determines your thinking.

Not only the lifestyle, but also your books determine your thinking.

Here, the verb agrees with the closest noun.

Time

Forty-five minutes is too long a break.

Five minutes were enough for me.

Some phrases are always in a particular number.

'One or more' and 'a number of' are plural.

Ensure that one or more options are selected.

A number of specialists are needed to complete the investigation.

However, 'the number of' is always singular.

The number of cells in your body keeps changing.

Gerund and infinitive phrases are always in the singular.

Going to plays is a great idea. (Gerund phrase)

To commit such crimes is frowned upon. (Infinitive phrase)

Exercise—Subject-verb agreement

Correct the following sentences:

1. Saroja as well as Padmini were great actors.
2. The gin and tonic were excellent.
3. The organiser, accompanied by some side-kicks, enter the auditorium.
4. Each bottle and can in the inventory need to be checked.
5. Either of you two have to win.
6. Either the pencil or the erasers is enough.
7. His unending invectives is the biggest problem.
8. The biggest problem are his unending invectives.
9. Is any of my books good?
10. If any of you answer the question, I'll be more than happy.
11. There are no pencil or books to write in.
12. There is no books or pencil to write with.
13. The jury ponder and reach a unanimous decision.
14. The couple lives in Jayanagar but go to work in different places.
15. He is one of those people who is always grumpy.
16. One of those people are very friendly.
17. A number of writers is mad.
18. The number of people in the club keep increasing.

Answers—Subject-verb agreement

Explanations have been given within brackets.

1. Saroja as well as Padmini was a great actor. (Here, 'Padmini' is an element that is not considered part of the subject.)

2. The gin and tonic was excellent. ('Gin and tonic' is treated as a single entity; therefore, it is treated as singular.)
3. The organiser, accompanied by some side-kicks, enters the auditorium. ('Some side-kicks' is not part of the main subject and hence, the verb agrees with 'The organiser', which is in singular form.)
4. Each bottle and can in the inventory needs to be checked. ('Each' and 'every' are normally treated individually and therefore, are in singular form.)
5. Either of you two has to win. ('Either' refers to one person here and hence, it is treated as singular.)
6. Either the pencil or the erasers are enough. (The closest noun is 'erasers', which is plural and therefore, the verb takes a plural form.)
7. His unending invectives are the biggest problem. (The subject 'invectives' is in plural form. Do not be misled by the singular 'problem'.)
8. The biggest problem is his unending invectives. (The subject here is 'problem', which is in singular form. Compare with the previous example.)
9. Are any of my books good?
10. If any of you answers the question, I'll be more than happy. (If the speaker means that one of them answering the question would make her happy, 'any' is in singular form.)
11. There is no pencil or books to write in. (With 'or', the verb takes the number of the closest noun, 'pencil', which is in singular form.)
12. There are no books or pencil to write with. (The verb takes the number of the closest noun, 'books', which is in plural form.)
13. The jury ponders and reaches a unanimous decision. (The verb takes a singular form as 'the jury' (a collective noun) acts as a single body.)
14. The couple live in Jayanagar but go to work in different places. (At least within the same sentence or in adjacent sentences, be consistent.)
15. He is one of those people who are always grumpy. (There are some 'people' who are grumpy. Therefore, the verb takes a plural form.)
16. One of those people is very friendly. (Refers to a single individual. Therefore, the verb takes a singular form.)

17. A number of writers are mad. ('A number of' always takes the plural form.)
18. The number of people in the club keeps increasing. ('The number of' always takes a singular form.)

Flawed parallelism

When the elements of a sentence are not consistent, it leads to faulty parallelism. This confuses the reader and distracts him from your narrative.

Let me illustrate parallelism with a few examples.

Examples

(Original, wrong) The lion was big, beautiful and growling.

In the above example, 'big' and 'beautiful' are adjectives, whereas 'growling' is a verb form (participle). All the elements in the list in the original sentence are not parallel.

(Revised) The lion was big and beautiful. It growled.

Now consider the following sentence:

(Original, wrong) He loved eating rather than walking and to host rather than attend.

In the above sentence, 'eating' and 'walking' are noun forms (gerunds) and 'to host' is a verb (an infinitive).

(Revised) He loved to eat rather than to walk and to host rather than to attend.

Consider a few more examples:

(Original, wrong) You can specialise in mathematics, drama, and in economics.

When you use a common preposition like 'in', either use it for all the elements in the list or use it once.

(Revised) You can specialise in mathematics, in drama, and in economics.

Or,

(Revised) You can specialise in mathematics, drama, and economics.

(Original, wrong) You can add or subtract items from the cart.

You add items to the cart, or you can subtract items from the cart. The above (original) sentence suggests that you can add items from the cart.

(Revised) You can either add to or subtract from the cart.

(Original, wrong) The restructuring calls for increased bonuses, budgets and smaller targets.

(Revised) The restructuring calls for increased bonuses and budgets and, in addition, smaller targets.

(Original, wrong) All members should indicate their preferences in the attached form and you should pick up your food coupon at the library.

(Revised) All members should indicate their preferences in the attached form and should pick up their food coupons at the library.

Exercise—Flawed parallels

Correct the errors in parallelism in the following sentences:

1. Go to the club office to change your address, phone number, or meet the secretary.
2. In an hour's time, he had not only read all his lessons but also a short story.
3. I like reading, writing and to sleep.
4. Watching too much television causes dizziness, loss of sleep, and you to be hungry.
5. He told me that he often chews gum, that he walks, he dances.
6. These are the following things you should avoid:
    - Telling rather than showing
    - Using adverbs indiscriminately
    - Add emotional baggage to dialogue tags
7. I can read fantasy, crime, and any novel of PG Wodehouse.
8. He likes chewing gum, cycling and to walk.
9. Quickly, and with great care, he made his presentation.
10. He feels neither happy, nor is he unhappy.

Answers—Flawed parallels

1. Go to the club office to meet the secretary or to change your address and phone number.

2. In an hour's time, he had read not only all his lessons but also a short story.
3. I like reading, writing, and sleeping.
4. Watching too much television causes dizziness, loss of sleep, and hunger.
5. He told me that he often chews gum, that he walks, that he dances.
6. These are the following things you should avoid:
    - Telling rather than showing
    - Using adverbs indiscriminately
    - Adding emotional baggage to dialogue tags
7. I can read fantasy, crime, and humour. I love PG Wodehouse in particular.
8. He likes chewing gum, cycling, and walking.
9. Quickly and carefully, he made his presentation.
10. He feels neither happy nor unhappy.

Confusion with conjunctions

Conjunctions are words that connect multiple clauses.

Examples include and, but, if, because, or.

Coordinate conjunctions

Coordinate conjunctions, the FANBOYS—for, and, nor, but, or, yet, and so—connect two independent clauses, which are parts of sentences that could stand alone, as in:

Karen loves ice cream, and she hates Marlene.

Subordinate conjunctions

Subordinate conjunctions, the WABBITS—when, where, while, after, although, before, because, if, though, since—connect a less important dependent clause to an independent clause, as in:

While Rome was burning, Nero was fiddling.

Here, 'Nero was fiddling' is the important clause, and 'Rome was burning' is the less important subordinate clause, connected by the conjunction 'while'.

Consider the following sentence:

(Original, wrong) After killing the dangerous dragons, rescuing the beautiful princesses, and claiming the magic wand, Arthur decided to walk back.

For a moment, forget the adjectives and concentrate on the primary intent in the sentence. The main clause describes Arthur deciding to walk back. Is that the part you would emphasise? All the important information has been subordinated.

A much better construction of the sentence would be to use another subordinating conjunction; this time, in your favour. You could recast the sentence thus:

(Revised) Before Arthur decided to walk back, he killed dangerous dragons, rescued beautiful princesses, and claimed the magic wand.

Note how the important stuff like killing dragons and rescuing princesses has subordinated Arthur's decision to walk back by the use of 'before'. Not that the sentence has lost its tackiness; that is another matter.

As a writer, you may even want to use the de-emphasising power of subordinating conjunctions to great effect, albeit in a quirky way.

Rasputin lost all touch with the Russian queen after he was poisoned, cut, shot, and drowned.

Conjunctions like 'and', 'but', 'or', and 'nor' give equal weight to the clauses they coordinate and therefore, they create fewer problems.

Conjunctions doing double duty

Beware of the conjunctions 'since', 'as', and 'while' because they are used in two different senses with the potential for confusion.

As

As I was working in the office the whole day, I was singing off-key.

Were you singing for the duration of your working in the office or was being in the office the cause for your off-key rendition, the office being one of those permissive ones where people are encouraged, nay, *required* to sing, particularly, off-key?

As I was working on the computer the whole day, I was doing my weights.

The problem here seems even more severe. 'As' can mean 'at the same time' (apart from 'because'). I should not be faulted for wondering how you worked on the computer and were doing your weights simultaneously.

While

'While' also creates a similar problem, since it normally implies simultaneity. You can also use it in the sense of 'although'.

While Rome was burning, Nero was fiddling.

It can mean either that Nero's fiddling and the burning of Rome happened simultaneously or in the sense of 'although'.

Since

Since Napoleon died, there have been no able generals.

Do you mean that there being no able generals is a direct result of Napoleon dying? Or do you mean that after Napoleon's death, there were not any good generals?

Double whammy

Each of the above conjunctions can cause a double whammy in a sentence. They can be at once ambiguous and give importance where not needed.

While Rasputin was the evil advisor, Alexandra was her regal self.

Importance is taken away from Rasputin. 'While' subordinates 'Rasputin was the evil advisor'. This may not have been the author's intention. An ambiguity also exists because of the two meanings of 'while'.

After, before

Before Ravi turned into a serial killer, he was a clerk.

Here, the interesting information about Ravi being a serial killer is de-emphasised because of the subordinating conjunction 'before'.

Until

Here is an example from an imaginary book blurb:

(Original, wrong) Until Alex Ganesh can slay the monster, rescue the princess, and claim the magic lamp, he cannot find peace.

Here, the main clause is 'he cannot find peace', and all the other interesting bits in the book have lost their importance.

(Revised) Alex Ganesh must slay the three-headed monster. Then he must marry the princess. He must then retrieve the magic lamp. Only then can he rest.

If

'If' has its own dangers, not necessarily to do with subordination.

Consider the following example:

> If you are fond of food, the Club kitchen has some great choices for you.

I presume that the kitchen has great choices, irrespective of your fondness for food.

Exercise – Subordinating conjunctions

Correct the following sentences, directing the emphasis where needed:

1. She got reasonable marks in Chemistry and Physics in the university examination, where she was placed first in the state.
2. Since the commander led from the front, the battalion won its battles.
3. Ramesh was a popular boy in class, before he started spraying ink on other students.
4. While he was writing the exams, he seemed unhappy.
5. Before he turned violent, he lived a normal life.
6. After she was declared the winner of the Nobel Prize, a lot of people congratulated her.
7. After kicking the door in, shooting the intruder in the face and freeing the princess, he felt hungry.
8. The soldier groaned as Arthur's dagger slashed across his neck and fell down.
9. While eating healthy food, don't talk.
10. If you are a member, the club offers great food.
11. Since you are a member of the club, could you tell me about the ambience?
12. Do you like golf more than your wife?

Answers – Subordinating conjunctions

There are many ways to skin a cat. First, you need to figure out whether skinning the cat will improve it. Leaving it alone might be wiser and far more humane. You can rewrite these sentences in many ways. I have suggested just one of them, or in a few cases, two of them.

1. The important part is that she was placed first in the state and that has got subordinated. A possible fix could be:

(Answer) She was placed first in the state, even though she only got reasonable marks in Chemistry and Physics.

2. The sentence is ambiguous. 'Since' has two meanings—'because' and 'from that time'. You might want to clarify your meaning.

(Answer) Because the commander led from the front, the battalion won many battles.

Or,

(Answer) Ever since the commander started leading from the front, the battalion won many battles.

3. In all probability, the important thing that is meant to be conveyed here is that Ramesh started spraying ink on fellow students. That information is getting subordinated here. You could try:

(Answer) Ramesh started spraying ink on other students; he was popular before that.

4. 'While' makes the sentence ambiguous. Was he unhappy during the examination? Or was he writing the examination although he was unhappy?

(Answer) Although he was unhappy, he wrote the examination.

Or,

(Answer) He was unhappy during his examination.

5. His turning violent might be the more important event, but it has got subordinated.

(Answer) He turned violent, and afterwards, his life was not the same.

6. Her 'winning the Nobel' is subordinated. Try:

(Answer) She won the Nobel Prize, and many people congratulated her.

7. Unless the writer was trying for comic effect, all the action—kicking the door in, shooting the intruder in the face, and freeing the princess—should be given importance over his feeling hungry.

(Answer) He kicked the door in. He shot the intruder in the face and rescued the swooning princess. He then realised he was hungry.

8. 'As' can mean 'because', or it can indicate simultaneity. It is a bit of a stretch for the soldier to receive a cut across the neck, all the while groaning and falling.

(Answer) Arthur's dagger slashed across his neck. The soldier groaned once and his body fell down.

9. (Answer) Concentrate on eating healthy (I can hear you say 'healthful') food, not on talking.

10. I think the club offers what it does regardless of your membership status.

(Answer) If you are a member, you can take advantage of the excellent food the club offers.

11. 'Since' makes the sentence ambiguous. Do you want the member to talk about the time after he joined the club or do you believe that because he is a member, he would be in a position to know?

(Answer) You must be familiar with the club because you are a member. How is the ambience?

Or,

(Answer) How is the club's ambience after you became a member?

The second form of the sentence could be mildly insulting to the person to whom it is addressed. The implication is that he had something to do with the club's ambience (possibly affected it badly) ever since he joined.

12. The question is ambiguous. The question could be about who likes golf better or the question may ask the listener to choose between golf and his (listener's) wife.

(Answer) What do you like better? Golf or your wife?

Or,

(Answer) Who likes golf better? You or your wife?

Anachronisms

These refer to events, people, or objects that appear before and after their time—typically from an earlier time.

A kid using a cassette recorder in the 2020s, for instance, is an example of a parachronism, where an object belonging to a much earlier era is used. Another type of anachronism is a prochronism, where the assigned date is earlier than the actual date.

Anachronisms in fiction

I had to be very careful about anachronisms when I wrote my historical fiction, which was set in the latter part of the 19th century. I had to make sure that even the expressions used pertained to that period. A tool that was very helpful for this purpose was the Google site: https://books.google.com/ngrams

Many dictionaries also have the first known use of a term.

For instance, I had to check whether the word 'unquote' was current in 1910. A quick check told me that it was not used until much later.

Even William Shakespeare has slipped up by introducing a prochronism.

Brutus: 'Peace! Count the clock.'

Cassius: 'The clock has stricken three.'

Act 2 Scene 1: *Julius Caesar*

In the novel *'Pride and Prejudice'* by Jane Austen, the characters sometimes use phrases that were not in common usage until much later. For example, the phrase 'I could not help but notice' was not used in its current form until the 19th century, while the novel is set in the late 18th century.

* * *

Wishes and demands

If wishes were horses, beggars would ride.

Old Scottish proverb

Writers often use the subjunctive mood ungrammatically. Some errors have even become mainstream.

The subjunctive mood is used for expressing various states of unreality, such as doubt, possibility, necessity, or action that is contrary to fact. It is also used to express situations that are desired.

In English, the subjunctive mood is used in clauses that begin with 'if' or 'that', and the sentence often contains the verb 'be' in the present tense, followed by the base form of the verb.

If I were you, I would take the job.

(The speaker is not actually you. The subjunctive mood is used to indicate that the action is hypothetical.)

(Wrong) I suggest that she is given the promotion.

(Corrected) I suggest that she be given the promotion.

The action of giving the promotion is not a fact, so the subjunctive mood is used to indicate that it is a suggestion or desire.

Except for the verb 'be', for all other verbs, the subjunctive forms are distinct only in the third person singular.

For instance, the third person singular present indicative of the verb 'take' is 'he'/ 'she'/ 'it takes'.

The subjunctive form is 'he'/'she'/'it take', as in:

The devil take him.

The subjunctive forms of the verb 'be' are given below:

Present Indicative	Present Subjunctive	Past Indicative	Past Subjunctive
I am	I be	I was	I were
You are	You be	You were	You were
He/She is	He/She be	He/She was	He/She were
We are	We be	We were	We were
They are	They be	They were	They were

A few examples of the subjunctive form are given below:

I wish I were a horse.

I insist that I be present.

I suggest that she be freed.

If wishes were horses, beggars would ride them.

Were we so inclined, we could have beaten them.

I command that they be reinstated with full back wages.

The boss insisted she stay back. (Past tense)

The following verbs usually take the subjunctive form:

- Recommend: It is recommended that he get out of the country.
- Insist: I insist that I be present at the gathering.
- Suggest: She suggested that they go to a park first.
- Demand: The teacher demanded that the students submit their

assignments on time.

- Request: We request that you provide us with the necessary instructions.
- Mandate: The law mandates that every citizen with a certain threshold income pay taxes.
- Advise: The lawyer advised that he take her recommendation.
- Urge: They urged that the government take immediate action.
- Order: The judge ordered that the defendant be freed.

The subjunctive may be disappearing. For instance:

'I wish I was a horse' is often considered correct.

Exercise—Subjunctive

Correct the following sentences:

1. I wish I was a bird.
2. The detective insisted that he came along.
3. The lawyer insisted that his client was seated.
4. I was certain that I were given VIP treatment.
5. If I was in the chorus, I would have sung.
6. If he was to follow me then, he would have had a shock.
7. I propose you are present at the meeting.
8. I must insist that she has a chance.
9. It is necessary that he uses the time allotted to him.
10. I suggest Ram reads a book.

Answers—Subjunctive

1. I wish I were a bird.
2. The detective insisted that he come along.
3. The lawyer insisted that his client be seated.
4. I was certain that I was given VIP treatment.
5. If I were in the chorus, I would have sung.
6. If he were to follow me then, he would have had a shock.
7. I propose that you be present at the meeting.
8. I must insist that she have a chance.
9. It is necessary that he use the time allotted to him.
10. I suggest Ram read a book.

Chapter 8
Complicated Sentences

Rule 8: Avoid Complexity

Consider the following passage:

> *In natural theology, where one conceives of an object that is not only not an object of intuition for us but cannot even be an object of sensible intuition for itself, one is careful to remove the conditions of time and space from all of its intuition (for all of its cognition must be intuition and not thinking, which is always proof of limitations). But with what right can one do this if one has antecedently made both of these into forms of things in themselves, and indeed ones that, as a priori conditions of the existence of things, would remain even if one removed the things themselves? - for as conditions of all existence in general they would also have to be conditions of the existence of God. If one will not make them into objective forms of all things, then no alternative remains but to make them into subjective forms of our kind of outer as well as inner intuition, which is called sensible because it is not original, i.e., one through which the existence of the object of intuition is itself given (and that, so far as we can have insight, can only pertain to the original being); rather it is dependent on the existence of the object, thus it is possible only insofar as the representational capacity of the subject is affected through that.*
>
> Emanuel Kant, *Critique of Pure Reason*

When you started reading the above, did you shake your head to clear it? Did you, like me, emerge from the passage with glazed eyes and a vacuous frown that threatens to last forever? Unless you are Kant and are writing for an appropriate reader, do not expect to pull off such a barrage of words.

When you use complicated sentences, you put readers off either because they cannot understand or because it slows their reading pace.

Why complexity?

You sound smart

During my early days of writing, I used to think I would sound smart if I used complex words and sentences. I know now that is not true.

On the contrary, a regular use of complex sentences shows a cluttered mind, not a clear one. If you write simple, clear prose, chances are that your thoughts will also become clearer, and a virtuous cycle will start, resulting in cleaner prose.

Great writing should be complex

Some feel that is the way all great literature should be written.

Again, this is not true at all. Do not judge by the style of the 19th and early 20th-century writers. The language they wrote was formal and reflected the mores of the society and culture. For an example of a great writer who could communicate a complex idea in simple but stylistic prose, think Kurt Vonnegut.

Complexity can make things concise

Let me not get into the merit of this statement. If complexity does come at the expense of conciseness, go ahead and be elaborate. Choose comprehensibility over conciseness every time.

How do sentences get complicated?

Complexity can arise from the use of:

- passive sentences
- misconnected sentences
- overly ornate prose (purple prose)
- redundancies
- other complex constructions, such as nouning the verb, using expletives, and nesting clauses deep

Passive sentences

The writing advice that is normally given is to avoid passive voice (particularly in non-academic writing).

Why is this so? In a passive sentence, the actor is optional. You give prominence to the thing to be acted upon and introduce the actor (if necessary) with a 'by'.

The man was murdered by a criminal gang. (Passive)

The man was murdered. (Passive, without the actor)

A criminal gang murdered the man. (Active)

Disadvantages of passive usage

Absence of clarity

If you use the passive voice, you may not have clarity about who is performing the action. This can make it unclear in many situations.

The man was killed.

The above passive construction leaves the part about who killed the man unclear.

Awkward word order

The natural word order in English is subject-verb-object. Active sentences follow this order. In passive sentences, the word order is object-verb-subject. This can make the sentence look stilted.

(Passive) The biscuit was eaten by the dog.

This looks awkward compared to:

(Active) The dog ate the biscuit.

Wordy

Passive sentences often sound wordy.

Compare the following two sentences:

The entrance was effected by the thief through the ventilator.

The thief entered through the ventilator.

Easy way out

Writers can take the easy way out when they do not know the actor, and this comes through when they try to get away with it by using the passive voice.

This meter bar was replaced in 1889 by thirty platinum-iridium bars kept across the globe.

Compare the above sentence with:

The International Geodetic Association replaced the meter bar in 1889 by thirty platinum-iridium bars kept across the globe.

When to use passive voice

Use passive voice when the truth of the sentence is universal, irrespective of the subject, and therefore, the actor is irrelevant.

Violence should be shunned.

The implied active sentence that sounds strange is:

Everyone should shun violence.

When the actor is unknown

The statue of Queen Victoria on Cubbon Road was defaced. (Passive)

Someone has defaced the statue of Queen Victoria on Cubbon Road. (Active)

As you can see, the passive version sounds better.

When you deliberately want the actor to be hidden

The boy said, 'All the chocolates have been eaten.'

When the emphasis is on the object and not the subject
Rather than writing 'Archaeologists discovered the figurine amidst the ruins', consider the following sentence:

The strange figurine was discovered amidst the ruins.

You want to leave it unclear if it was a shepherd boy or an archaeologist who found it because that is not the main point of the sentence.

Scientific papers often use passive voice to keep the focus on the experiment and not on the researcher. Researchers also use it in academic writing to avoid the use of 'I'.

The DNA was then isolated.

(Gendered) If a critic wants to critique a book, he has to first buy it.

If you use the passive voice, you can avoid the use of the gendered pronoun 'he'.

(Inclusive) If a book needs to be critiqued, the critic should first buy it.

Conversion from passive to active

(Passive—Original) When it was clear the access was gained by the thief through the ventilator, it was ordered by the king to have all the ventilators sealed.

(Active—Solution) The king discovered that the thief had entered through the ventilator. He ordered that all ventilators be sealed.

Exercise—Active/passive constructions

Change the following into active sentences where needed:

1. It is used in academic writing.
2. The consequences have to be faced by you.
3. The pen has been stolen.
4. The pen is lost.
5. Not only were the horses injured, but the king also was hurt.
6. A person can be pushed only thus far and no farther.
7. I see that four dots have been used by you at the end of the sentence.
8. She noticed that hair had just started sprouting atop his head.
9. He was congratulated by all.
10. They have been instructed to kick the sack at regular intervals.
11. He was hit by an arrow.

Answers—Active/passive constructions

1. It is used in academic writing. (Leave it as it is.)
2. You have to face the consequences.
3. The pen has been stolen. (Leave it as it is.)
4. The pen is lost. (Leave it be as it is already in the active voice.)
5. Not only were the horses injured, but the king also was hurt. (Leave it be; we do not know who did all this.)
6. You can push a person only thus far and no farther.
7. I see that you have used four dots at the end of the sentence.
8. She noticed that hair had just started sprouting atop his head. (It is already in the active voice).
9. Everyone congratulated him.
10. They have been instructed to kick the sack at regular intervals. (Leave it be; we do not know who has given the instructions.)
11. An arrow hit him.

Misconnected sentences

These are presented in the order of increasing sin.

Comma splice

A comma splice occurs when you connect two complete sentences with just a comma instead of a conjunction.

(Wrong) I read every day, I need to sleep properly.

To fix this, use a conjunction or (less frequently) a semicolon.

(Corrected) Because I read every day, I need to sleep properly.

Or,

(Corrected) I read every day; I need to sleep properly.

Run-on sentences

A run-on sentence occurs when two complete sentences are connected improperly without using a conjunction or appropriate punctuation.

(Wrong) I could do this all day long I just need the energy.

(Correct) I could do this all day long; I just need the energy.

(Correct) I could do this all day long. I just need the energy.

(Correct) I could do this all day long if I had the energy.

Disparate sentences

(Wrong) I read every day and I ate two slices of bread today.

These two sentences are problematic even without connecting them into a single sentence. There is no relationship between the sentences. To make some kind of logic, you can put them in different paragraphs, or at least explain why you put them together in the first place.

(Correct) I read every day and today I ate two slices of bread instead.

Or,

(Correct) I read every day, and today I ate two slices of bread during that time.

Purple prose

Identifying purple prose

Purple prose is characterised by an overly ornate language, with some or many of the features below:

- run-on sentences
- long clauses piled one on top of the other
- words of many syllables
- fanciful adjective-noun pairs
- a number of adverbs
- unnecessary and often tacky metaphors and similes

Example of purple prose:

> The dexterous dwarf gingerly lifted up the delicate crystal goblet, casting a doleful eye around for sundry desperate dragons, his countenance dark and enigmatic like a thundercloud at night, he seriously contemplated dropping the object of power into the dark cavernous depths of the wishing well, wondering all the time whether it would appear seemly, the ancient wizard might appear unexpectedly betime. He was as undecided as a desert lizard on the boiling hot crags of an old active volcano.

Let us analyse the above piece of over-the-top (exaggerated) purple prose, even for a constructed example.

Use of nauseating adjective-noun pairs:

- dexterous dwarf
- delicate crystal goblet
- doleful eye
- sundry dragons
- cavernous depths
- ancient wizard

Adjectives galore:

- dexterous (alliterative to boot)
- doleful
- dark
- enigmatic
- dark, cavernous

Note the use of multiple adjectives for the same noun, as in: delicate crystal, old active.

Adverbs:

- gingerly
- seriously
- seemly
- unexpectedly

Tacky metaphors/similes:

- dark and enigmatic, like a thundercloud at night

- undecided as a desert lizard on the boiling hot crags of an old active volcano

A run-on sentence:
'He seriously contemplated ...' deserves to be a separate sentence by itself (in as much as it deserves to be there at all).

Pretentious words:

- betime
- seemly

Problems with purple prose

Purple prose can be difficult to understand. It also draws attention to itself, and if the hype created by the words is not justified by the content, it falls flat.

Redundant words and phrases

Writing concisely without compromising the meaning enhances the quality of your work. There are a couple of words that you can do away with altogether. Just write 'think' instead of 'think to yourself' and 'gift' instead of 'free gift'. See Appendix 2 for more examples.

Unnecessary prepositions

The prepositions in the following cases can be (and sometimes must be) dropped altogether:

cope up, clean up, enter into, escape from, finish up,
flee from, jump up, miss out, meet up, orbit around,
permeate through, shout out, sit down, start off,
separate out, browse through, join together

Other redundant phrases

as per (per), both agree (agree), collide into each other (collide),
crammed close together (crammed), a little bit (a bit),
hotter temperature (hotter—or higher temperature),
colder temperature (colder—or lower temperature),
used to in the past (used to),
wander around aimlessly (wander, roam)

Verb-noun combinations

Often, a verb can be used instead of a verb-noun combination:

have a drink (drink)
have food (eat)
pay attention (concentrate)
pay a visit (visit)
make progress (improve)
make a statement (state)
make a mistake (err)
make a mess (mess up)
come to a decision (decide)
got the sack (sacked)
get upset (upset)
go sailing (sail)
do the washing-up (wash-up)
take a look (look)
take risk (risk)
give advice (advise)

In legalese:

indemnify and hold harmless
last will and testament

Exercise—Redundancy

Cut the deadwood from the following sentences:

1. As to whether he will actually do it, I do not know for certain.
2. We both agreed that it was pointless.
3. The lion was wandering around aimlessly when it found what he was looking for, a prey.
4. The temperature gets really hot in deserts.
5. It has not gone unnoticed that your performance has really improved.
6. I cannot cope up with all these troubles.
7. Let us escape from this madness, sit down in a quiet, noiseless corner and really sort it out.
8. He missed out on his home food.
9. The moon orbits around the Earth even while the Earth orbits

around the sun.

10. That is all past history.
11. We have come to the decision that we are going to sack you.

Answers—Redundancy

1. I am not sure whether he will do it.
2. We agreed it was pointless.
3. The lion was wandering when it found the prey.
4. It gets hot in deserts.
5. We see your performance has improved.
6. I cannot cope with all these troubles.
7. Let us escape this madness, sit in a quiet corner, and sort it.
8. He missed his home food.
9. The moon orbits the Earth, while the Earth orbits the sun.
10. That is all history.
11. We have decided to sack you.

Nominalisation

Verbing the noun at least contributes to conciseness. Often, it also becomes mainstream. For instance:

Let me email you. Then you can table the topic.

Nouning the verb, also called nominalisation, is worse. It invariably leads to longer sentences. You would have noticed by now that nominalisation itself is a nominalisation.

By using nominalisations (forming a noun from a verb or an adjective), you can create awkward sentences.

(Too long) Kalyan had showed/exhibited happiness.

(Corrected) Kalyan was happy.

(Bad) The singing of the song triggered unhappy memories in me.

(Corrected) The song triggered unhappy memories in me.

Nominalisations are wordy. They convert an action into an inanimate object or an abstraction, and they downplay the doer of an action.

One part of speech for the other

Often, some of these efforts find their way into the language permanently.

Verbing a noun: Don't keep texting me.

Nouning a verb: That was an epic fail.

Adjectivising a noun: a genius idea

Nouning an adjective: eating weird, I love funny

More complicated sentences

Expletives

Expletives are phrases of the form 'it + be-verb' or 'there + be-verb'. Such expressions can be appropriate in speech and for emphasis in some situations but create overblown prose. They are wordy and sound overly dramatic.

Examples:

(Wordy) It is the thief who took the watch.

(Corrected) The thief took the watch.

(Wordy) It is I who is to blame.

(Corrected) I am to blame.

Other wordy usages

Avoid usages like:

(Original) He was the kind of man who expected his breakfast on time.

(Revised) He expected his breakfast on time.

Exercise—Expletives

Make the following sentences concise:

1. It is the purpose that is important.
2. It was the school principal who gave away the prizes.
3. There was a sound heard, and people rushed to see what happened.
4. She was the kind of author who, like me, uses complex words to convey a simple thought.

Answers—Expletives

1. The purpose is important.
2. The school principal gave away the prizes.
3. People rushed to see what the sound was about.

4. The author, like me, uses complex words to convey a simple thought.

Other complex constructions

If you do not keep subjects and objects close to their verbs, you are likely to get confusing sentences.

> Unwrapping a piece of gum, complacent in the belief that the enemy, considered notoriously inept, was probably around sucking a lollipop, Clouseau popped it into his mouth.

In the sentence given above, you encounter the subject (Clouseau) after such a long gap that you would have to read the sentence again to figure out what he popped into his mouth. Was it a lollipop or maybe a piece of the enemy?

Keep Clouseau close to the gum and you should be okay. Do not let a reader fret and fume in your waiting room till you call.

Only and Always

When you use 'only' or 'always', place them next to the words they modify.

> (Original) You are only required to do twenty push-ups in one sitting.

(The truth was, you needed to do 50 sit-ups too, something more appropriate to do in a sitting.)

> (Revised) You are required to do only twenty push-ups in one sitting.

This allows the possibility of springing other unpleasant facts, like the sit-ups that need to be done.

'Only' and 'always' can function anywhere in the sentence, altering the meaning every time. You will, therefore, need to position these carefully. Consider the following sentence:

> Marlene had ice cream with noodles.
>
> Only Marlene had ice cream with noodles. (No one else could be so eccentric.)
>
> Marlene had only ice cream with noodles. (Normally, she has other things, like Tabasco sauce, with her noodles.)
>
> Marlene had ice cream with only noodles. (She would normally eat other things as well with her ice cream, for instance, pickles.)
>
> Always, Marlene had only ice cream and noodles. (Whenever she sat down to eat, Marlene ate ice cream and noodles.)

Which comes first, the main clause or conditions?

(Original, incorrect) If, and only if, you want to be compared to a not-too-prosperous farmer out on a holiday to meet his childhood sweetheart of a decade or an axe murderer, escaped from the prison on the loose, should you wear plaids.

Don't write thus, unless you want your character to be established as a pompous ass. Do the reader a favour. Put the main clause first, if there is a long conditional clause.

(Corrected) If you wear plaids, you will be compared to a not-too-prosperous farmer out on a holiday to meet his childhood sweetheart of a decade or an axe murderer on the loose from prison.

Do not nest them deep

Here is a really horrid sentence:

Ramon, who wrote a book on the Peacock Throne, whose books, some of which were obscure, were acknowledged by some, especially those, who were considered connoisseurs of writing that mirrors the social milieus as brilliant, yet eccentric, died.

You nest them deep; the reader will be lost in the maze. I wonder, too, whether Ramon actually died on the Peacock Throne. Someone died. Perhaps a writer or, more likely, a reader.

Exercise—Complex constructions

Untangle the following sentences:

1. The king, whose prowesses on the battlefield, particularly in that ill-fated battle of Doddachikkanahalli, were well- known, slept peacefully despite what was to come.
2. If you want to be acknowledged by one and all as an important writer in an already crowded field, write more.

Answers—Complex constructions

1. The king slept peacefully despite what was to come; he was confident about his well-known prowesses on the battlefield — for instance, in that ill-fated battle of Doddachikkanahalli.
2. Write more, if you want to be acknowledged by one and all as an important writer in an already crowded field.

When to use a complex construction

You might use a complex construction just to provide a variety and balance. See the examples given below:

> *When we see men grow old and die at a certain time one after another, from century to century, we laugh at the elixir that promises to prolong life to a thousand years; and with equal justice may the lexicographer be derided, who being able to produce no example of a nation that has preserved their words and phrases from mutability, shall imagine that his dictionary can embalm his language, and secure it from corruption and decay, that it is in his power to change sublunary nature, and clear the world at once from folly, vanity, and affectation.*

SAMUEL JOHNSON: PREFACE TO HIS *DICTIONARY OF THE ENGLISH LANGUAGE* (1755)

> *It will, no doubt, be given to our countrymen of future generations to serve India by their successes; we, of the present generation, must be content to serve her mainly by our failures; for, hard though it be, out of those failures the strength will come, which in the end will accomplish great tasks.*

BIPIN CHANDRA QUOTING GOKHALE IN *INDIA SINCE INDEPENDENCE.*

Rhetoric and Figures of Speech

Let me begin by distinguishing between rhetoric and figures of speech. Rhetoric is the art of using language to persuade through written or spoken communication. It involves the use of various techniques, such as appealing to the audience's emotions or using logical arguments to influence the way people think or act.

Figures of speech, on the other hand, are expressions that use words in a non-literal or imaginative way in order to create a particular effect or meaning. Examples of figures of speech include metaphors, similes, and hyperbole.

While figures of speech can be used in a rhetorical technique, they are not the same as rhetoric. Rhetoric encompasses a wide range of strategies and techniques, while figures of speech are a specific type of language device.

Figures of speech work brilliantly in poetry. They work well in prose, too, but you have to be more careful in their usage. Appropriate metaphors, in particular, can elevate the quality of writing and make it stand out.

Please do read *The Second Coming* by WB Yeats if you have not done so already. This is a poem that has contributed to more book and movie titles than any other.

For instance:

- *Things Fall Apart* by Chinua Achebe
- *The Second Coming* by Walker Percy
- *The Center Cannot Hold: My Journey Through Madness* (2007) by Elyn Saks

Do not misuse rhetorical devices in writing. They can sound overly dramatic.

While they are energising in formal speeches, they are often an overkill in the written form.

Here are a few types of rhetoric/figures of speech. I have explained some of the more common ones here. The remaining are in Appendix 3.

Irony

Irony is the use of words to describe something other than that shown by their literal meaning, often the opposite of what they imply. Here is an example of irony:

For Brutus is an honourable man;

So are they all, all honourable men–

Come I to speak in Caesar's funeral.

He was my friend, faithful and just to me–

But Brutus says he was ambitious;

And Brutus is an honourable man.

WILLIAM SHAKESPEARE, *JULIUS CAESAR*

When Mark Antony says, 'Brutus is an honourable man', he means the opposite.

Verbal irony, with which we are concerned here, can be:

A sentence that means the opposite of what it apparently says.

'You have a surprise quiz now,' said the teacher.

'Isn't that great?' said Mark.

Pretending to be ignorant

'I thought you were starting the show at 10 am. Isn't it 11 am now?'

Overstating the case (use of hyperbole)

'I'll faint dead if you don't give me a drink now.'

Understating the case

It was a confusion of ideas between him and one of the lions he was hunting in Kenya that caused A.B. Spottsworth to make the obituary column. He thought the lion was dead, and the lion thought it wasn't.

PG WODEHOUSE, *RING FOR JEEVES.*

Metaphors and similes

Metaphors and similes both compare things. While in metaphors, the comparison is implicit, a simile explicitly uses a word such as 'like'.

Good metaphors and similes can make the writing evocative.

The sun was an orange ball.

Sometimes, appropriate metaphors set the mood for the passage.

The sky was a purple bruise.

Complex concepts, such as scientific ones, can be explained simply through a metaphor.

There is a story, probably apocryphal, about Lord Byron. In an examination where he was supposed to discuss the miracle of Christ turning water into wine, he wrote nothing on his paper for two hours and finally wrote this sentence: 'Water saw its master and blushed.'

Metaphors are a double-edged sword. If you use them badly, you can turn off the reader.

Here is an extended metaphor.

And all the men and women merely players;
They have their exits and their entrances;
And one man in his time plays many parts,
His acts being seven ages...

WILLIAM SHAKESPEARE, *AS YOU LIKE IT*

Here is a simile.

This was a fairly pretty girl, except that she had legs like an Edwardian grand piano.

KURT VONNEGUT, *SLAUGHTERHOUSE- FIVE*

Metaphors to avoid

Clichéd metaphors

Her eyes were twin stars.

He is a shining star.

The snow is a white blanket.

Double-edged sword (Oops! I just used it a while back.)

Anachronistic metaphors

'Let them eat cake,' said Marie Antoine, telegraphing her attitude in just four words.

(OK, so she might not have actually said it, but that is not the point. The telegraph, surely, had not been invented then.)

Mixed metaphors

Do you expect the lion of Punjab to bell the cat?
Don't throw stones at sleeping dogs from glass houses.
He drew the short straw, but that was the last straw.
We have our backs against a wall. Let's face up to it.
Are you a man or a mouse? If I were you, I would smell a rat.

Unless, of course, you are doing it for comic effect, as in:

I am shooting from the seat of my pants.

Inappropriate metaphors

She grew on him like a rash.

Let's bite the bullet and do some straight shooting.

On the other hand, the shoe is on the other foot.

Sometimes, you do it to lend a touch of humour.

That the author of the reminiscences should be writing scurrilous stories about him with one hand and strolling calmly into his private study, with, so to speak, the other, occasioned him the keenest resentment.

PG WODEHOUSE, *SUMMER LIGHTNING*

PG Wodehouse shows his comic intent by adding the phrase 'so to speak' in this deliberately clumsy metaphor.

Stretching metaphors beyond the breaking point

Children are like plants. Parenting is like tending to them. Don't pull them out by the roots to make them grow; just give them the right environment.

(So far, I am doing fine, but when I stretch it further, it breaks.)

The way organic fertiliser is best for plants... (you get the drift.)

Complex, difficult to follow metaphors/similes

He knew how the electron must have felt during a quantum entanglement.

Similes are metaphors with sibling envy.

The same caveats apply to similes, too. For instance, don't write:

The infants looked at each other like an antibody would eye an antigen.

It was worse than being back in a Little Lord Fauntleroy suit and ringlets and having a keen-eyed nurse always at one's elbow, watching one's every move like a bally hawk.

PG WODEHOUSE, *JEEVES AND THE FEUDAL SPIRIT*

Metonymy and synecdoche

Substituting an attribute (or anything closely connected) for the original thing is metonymy. Substituting a part for the whole is synecdoche.

Examples of metonymy

'The crown' for 'the King'

'Pen' for 'written material' (as in 'the pen is mightier than the sword'.)

'Press' for 'news organisations'

Examples of synecdoche

'wheels' instead of 'car'

'head' instead of 'a person'

'hands' instead of 'workers'

'boots' instead of 'soldiers'

Oxymoron

Oxymoron is a figure of speech where you use contrary terms side-by-side. This creates an apparent contradiction. The word 'oxymoron' itself is made up of two words that mean 'sharp' or 'pointed' and 'dull' or 'stupid'. Thus, the word 'oxymoron' itself is an oxymoron. Examples include:

preposterous: pre = before, posterior = hind part

upside-down, head over heels

Many oxymorons are made up of adjective-noun combinations.

A well-known example is from William Shakespeare's *Romeo and Juliet*.

O heavy lightness, serious vanity,
Misshapen chaos of well-seeming forms!
Feather of lead, bright smoke, cold fire, sick health,
Still-waking sleep, that is not what it is!
This love feel I, that feel no love in this.

Or, in *Macbeth*:

Fair is foul, and foul is fair.

Sounds of Silence is a song by Paul Simon— the title itself is oxymoronic. Look at the oxymoron in:

Some mute inglorious Milton here may rest,
Some Cromwell guiltless of his country's blood.

ELEGY WRITTEN IN A COUNTRY CHURCHYARD BY THOMAS GRAY

Mahatma Gandhi made a watchword of an oxymoron—Satyagraha.

The 'great little dictionary' is another example.

Comic potential of oxymorons

You can infuse a comic element where there was none before, by calling a phrase an 'oxymoron'.

For instance, if you call British intelligence an oxymoron, the implication is that being British and being intelligent are contradictory to each other.

The same holds for 'honest politician'. In fact, you can take any adjective-common noun combination and call it an oxymoron, often with comical effect.

Paradox

A paradox is a figure of speech where a statement contradicts itself.

'Some day you will be old enough to start reading fairy tales again.'

CS Lewis

One of the tenets in Bernard Shaw's *Man and Superman* reads as:

The golden rule is that there is no golden rule.

Thoreau had written:

Nothing is so much to be feared as fear,

and Franklin Delano Roosevelt had popularised it with his inaugural speech:

So, first of all, let me assert my firm belief that the only thing we have to fear is... fear itself — nameless, unreasoning, unjustified terror which paralyses needed efforts to convert retreat into advance.

I am talking about literary paradoxes here and not about logical paradoxes.

Paraprosdokian

A paraprosdokian is a figure of speech in which the latter part of a clause, sentence, or paragraph springs a surprise, and you have to re-evaluate the meaning. It is used often in comedy. Some examples are given below:

There are three kinds of people in the world–those who can count, and those who can't.

Anon

When I was a kid, my parents moved a lot, but I always found them.

Rodney Dangerfield

If all the girls who attended the Yale prom were laid end to end, I wouldn't be a bit surprised.

Dorothy Parker

He taught me housekeeping; when I divorce, I keep the house.

ZsaZsa Gabor

'Hah, I will tell you what poetry is. You know what a haiku is?' asked Dwipada.

'A high-level plot to dethrone the king?' Ponni hazarded a guess.

'It is a form of Eastern poetry,' said Bana with a superior air.

'That's right. Here's a rare example. A very rare one. A guru-brother taught me this—

'Thunder booms.

The swallow spreads its white speckled wings; Without concern.

And flies away.'

'What does that mean?' Bana burst out. 'Also, a haiku is supposed to be exactly seventeen syllables long. This one is far too long.'

'How perceptive,' said Dwipada. 'This is exactly why it is rare.'

D. KALYANARAMAN, *SORCERER OF MANDALA*

Chapter 9
Ambiguous Sentences

Rule 9: Mean What You Say

An ambiguous sentence is one that can mean more than one thing. You can, on occasion, use ambiguity as a deliberate tool as well.

You should avoid unintended ambiguity in your words and sentences. Sometimes, the reason for ambiguity is not clear. I had sent a copy of the book you are holding now to a well-known critic for a few sound bites. Here is what she wrote:

> 'I can't tell you how much I enjoyed reading the book. I can't recommend this book too strongly. I can't say which I like better, his humour or the prose. The book seems to have that page-turning quality. I finished reading it in an hour. I just cannot compare *Write Like A Pro* to any other book. He writes about ambiguity with some great examples. I would even say that the whole book serves as a great example.'

A friend of mine thought the critique was ambiguous. I didn't. That brings me to the idea that ambiguity is very often resolved in a given context. That is why words can afford to have multiple meanings. For instance, the word 'set' has over 400 meanings.

True ambiguity happens when you can interpret the meaning in more than one way in the context in which the word appears.

Consider the following sentence:

The fisherman rowed the boat towards the opposite bank.

You can be reasonably certain that the writer does not mean the fisherman intended to deposit his catch at the State Bank of India.

Dangling things

One source of ambiguity is the dangling participle or dangling modifier.

Dangling things can be made to a template. (Don't attempt it at home!)

Modifying clause/phrase (with an implied actor) with a modifier + new actor + main clause

This template is almost a certain recipe for disaster. Let me explain. Consider the following sentence:

While writing the book, the electric power went off.

Let us look at the following fragments:

Fragment 1—While writing the book

Fragment 2—the electric power

Fragment 3—went off.

Fragment 1 is the modifying clause. It contains the participle 'writing'—a present participle. There is no actor explicitly specified here. In other words, the sentence does not specify who is writing the book. A normal understanding would be that the person doing the writing is 'I'.

Fragment 2 is the decoy actor. It is just a noun that happens to be in the wrong place. With the decoy actor, 'I' is no longer the person here.

Fragment 3 is the additional action that is performed. Is the electric power writing the book? 'Writing' (a participle) now dangles forlornly between two actors. This is an example of a dangling participle.

Dangling modifier

Dangling modifiers can also be made to the same template. Consider the following sentence:

With over 120 years of experience, I can trust Tata Steel to make good steel.

Fragment 1—With over 120 years of experience

Fragment 2—I

Fragment 3—can trust Tata Steel to make good steel.

Fragment 1 is the modifying clause and hence, the modifier. There is no actor explicitly stated here.

In Fragment 2, 'I' is the decoy actor. Again, it is a noun (well, a pronoun in this case) in the wrong place.

Fragment 3 specifies the action. The '120 years of experience' obviously cannot be mine. The modifier is left dangling as before.

Other examples
After joining the MNC, her fortune turned.

She was the one who presumably went to work for an MNC, not her fortune.

Upon opening the garage door, a colony of bats flew out.

Somehow, I don't think the bats managed to open the garage door.

Exercise—Dangling things

Undangle the following sentences:

1. Rummaging through the purse, the money was missing.
2. Driving to the station, an accident happened.
3. Wanting to impress everyone around, the magic trick was performed and was a great success.
4. A dangling modifier walks into a bar. After finishing the drink, the bartender asks it to leave.
5. One morning, I shot an elephant in my pyjamas. (Groucho Marx, in *Animal Crackers,* goes on to say, 'How he got it in my pyjamas, I shall never know.')
6. Upon joining the army, the recruiter had a medical test for me.
7. Upon entering the museum, a dinosaur caught my eye.
8. Climbing up to the balcony, Juliet's cat was saved.
9. The witness described the thief as masked, with thick eyebrows weighing around a hundred kilos.

Answers—Dangling things

1. Rummaging through the purse, I saw that the money was missing.
2. Driving to the station, I ran into an accident.
3. Wanting to impress everyone around, she performed the magic trick and was a great success.
4. A dangling modifier walks into a bar. After the modifier finishes the drink, the bartender asks it to leave.
5. One morning, I shot an elephant that was wearing my pyjamas. (Or more realistically, one morning, while I was wearing my pyjamas, I shot an elephant.)
6. Upon my joining the army, the recruiter had a medical test for me.
7. Upon entering the museum, I saw a dinosaur.

8. Climbing up to the balcony, Romeo saved Juliet's cat.
9. The witness described the thief as weighing around a hundred kilos, masked, with thick eyebrows.

Misplaced modifiers

Misplaced modifiers modify unintended targets. Usually, this is because the modifier is separated from the modified.

(Original) We asked all writers to attend a meeting on Wednesday.

Did you ask on Wednesday or was the meeting on Wednesday? If the intention was to say that you had asked on Wednesday, I am afraid that does not get communicated because 'asked' and 'on Wednesday' are too far apart.

(Corrected) We asked all writers to attend a meeting scheduled on Wednesday.

Or,

(Corrected) On Wednesday, we asked all writers to attend a meeting.

The first sentence means that the meeting is on Wednesday, and the second sentence means that the writers were asked on Wednesday.

Students will be chastised for their taste in dressing, low scores and unauthorised absences. (Misplaced)

Obviously, students will not be chastised for their taste in low scores or their taste for unauthorised absences.

Going up stairs quickly gets you into a good condition. (Misplaced)

Does going up stairs very fast improve your fitness or does it improve the fitness rapidly?

Exercise—Misplaced modifiers

Help the misplaced modifiers in the following sentences to find their way:

1. The thief snatched at the pink woman's purse.
2. He wanted to possess the fat man's wallet.
3. The soldier in full uniform saluted and gave his reports. The general wanted more details from the bald soldier's statement.
4. They ate the biscuits that they had bought from the bakery hurriedly.
5. The man served a dosa to the woman that was round, golden and well-buttered.

Answers—Misplaced modifiers

1. The thief snatched at the woman's pink purse.
2. He wanted to possess the man's fat wallet.
3. The soldier in full uniform saluted and gave his reports. The general wanted more details rather than the soldier's bald statement.
4. They hurriedly ate the biscuits that they had bought from the bakery.
5. The man served to the woman a dosa that was round, golden and well-buttered.

Squinting modifiers

Squinting modifiers are more difficult to identify as they seem fine at the first glance. They are ambiguous. You cannot be certain what they modify.

(Original) The leader said on Wednesday we'd have to eat all the food that's been ordered.

There are two possible meanings of the sentence given above:

- The leader said this on Wednesday.
- Eat all the ordered food on Wednesday.

Both are equally possible.

(Corrected) 'We'd have to eat all the food that's been ordered,' the leader said on Wednesday.

(Corrected) 'On Wednesday, we'd have to eat all the food that's been ordered,' the leader said..

Exercise—Squinting modifiers

Correct the squint in the following sentences:

1. Walking up the stairs rapidly strengthens your leg muscles.
2. Boiling the milk slowly changes the nutrition content.
3. Drinking milk often helps those with vitamin deficiencies.
4. I told her this morning I was coming.
5. To weep sometimes is manly.
6. The book that you gave me yesterday went missing.
7. Writing often is satisfying.

Answers—Squinting modifiers

1. Walking up the stairs strengthens your leg muscles rapidly.

Or,

Rapidly walking up the stairs strengthens your leg muscles.

2. Boiling the milk changes the nutrition content slowly.

Or,

Slowly boiling the milk changes the nutrition content.

3. Frequently drinking milk helps those with vitamin deficiencies.

Or,

Sometimes, drinking milk helps those with vitamin deficiencies.

4. This morning, I told her I was coming.

Or,

I told her I was coming this morning.

5. To weep once in a while is manly.

Or,

To weep is manly sometimes.

6. The book that you gave me went missing yesterday.

Or,

The book that you gave me yesterday went missing.

7. Writing is satisfying when done often.

Or,

Often, writing is satisfying.

Unclear antecedents

An antecedent is a noun represented by a pronoun. We use pronouns like he, she, I, we, her, and me instead of a noun, usually to avoid repeating a noun. An unclear antecedent happens when you are not clear which noun the pronoun is referring to.

As the police chief fired at the fleeing criminal, he fell dead.

Who died? Does the pronoun 'he' refer to the police chief or the fleeing criminal? It is not clear.

John told Andy he was planning to commit suicide. He resolved immediately to inform a police officer. He died soon after.

What did John say? Did he say that John would commit suicide, or was he referring to Andy? Who informed the police? Who died? John, Andy, or the police officer?

Using the pronoun before the antecedent

You should make it clear to the reader which antecedent stands for which noun.

Did you see what I just did there? I used 'it' before specifying its antecedent. Don't write thus. Don't create a suspense where none is needed.

Or, for instance,

If your phone is now fixed, send me a message.

Exercise—Unclear antecedents

Identify the problems in the following sentences and correct them if needed.

1. I kept my ring in the car, and now it's gone.
2. The speakers kept droning on. The crowd was getting restive. One of them left. Why would that happen?
3. Parvathy told her sister that she had an ingrown toenail.
4. If it is not kept in the freezer, the food will lose the aroma.
5. When the police officer tackled the thief, he thought he broke his ankle.
6. I walked my dog and then picked up my sister from her friend's place before she got hungry.
7. Make a noise like an egg and beat it. (PG Wodehouse, *Clicking of Cuthbert and Other Stories*)

Answers—Unclear antecedents

The problems are identified in what follows.

1. Does the 'it' refer to the ring or car? It is an ambiguous reference to an antecedent.

   (Corrected) I had kept my ring in the car, and now the ring's gone.

   Or,

   (Corrected) I had kept my ring in the car, and now the car's gone.

2. What does 'that' in the last sentence refer to? The droning, the crowd's getting restive, or one of them leaving?

(Corrected) The speakers kept droning on. The crowd was getting restive. One of them left. Why would the speakers keep doing that?

3. Who had an ingrown toenail? Parvathy or her sister?

(Corrected) Parvathy had an ingrown toenail. She told her sister about it.

4. The pronoun 'it' is used before its antecedent, 'food'.

While the sentence is not strictly ambiguous, it is better reworded thus: (Corrected) The food will lose the aroma if it is not kept in the freezer.

5. Who broke the ankle? The police officer or the thief? The antecedent is ambiguous.

(Corrected) The police officer thought he broke his ankle when he caught the thief.

6. Who got hungry, the dog or my sister? This is an ambiguous antecedent.

(Corrected) I walked my dog. I then picked up my sister before she got hungry, from her friend's place.

7. Leave it be. I would not dare correct the master. He has deliberately used the pronoun as though it had an antecedent.

Another kind of ambiguity

Visiting friends can be fun.

This sentence can mean two things: Going to visit friends can be fun or friends who visit can be fun. Is it a gerund or a modifier? Similarly,

Flying drones can be dangerous.

Playing cards can be fun.

How to undangle lost modifiers

There is more than one way to untangle modifiers. The fundamental ways are:

1. Make the actor in the modifying phrase/clause explicit.
2. Make sure that the first noun that is encountered after the modifying phrase is the implicit actor in the modifier.

Exercise—Ambiguity

Correct the danglers, if any, in the following sentences:

1. While playing with the cricket ball, the mobile rang.
2. Although the heartthrob of millions, Sanjay's mind refused to accept

the accolades.

3. Having been shouted at for laziness, a computer was what Alice needed to make her productive.
4. Driving down MG Road, the Barton centre was seen.
5. As a student, the detention room was his zone of solace.
6. First out of the classroom, getting home was Rizvan's main priority.
7. Once over the enemy territory, military strategists forecast trouble for the aircraft.
8. Even with a brilliantly written term paper, the teacher refused additional marks to Kim.

Answers—Ambiguity

1. While he was playing with the cricket ball, the cellphone rang.
2. Although Sanjay was the heartthrob of millions, his mind refused to accept the accolades.
3. Having been shouted at for laziness, Alice needed a computer to make her productive.
4. Driving down MG Road, she saw the Barton centre.
5. As a student, he found solace in the detention room.
6. First out of the classroom, Rizvan prioritised getting home.
7. Once the planes are over the enemy territory, strategists forecast trouble for the aircraft.
8. Even though Kim had written a brilliant term paper, the teacher refused to award additional marks to her.

Vague and imprecise writing

It helps if you sound as though you know what you are saying. Your hedging statements do not help your authenticity. You don't have to state that something is approximate, that on closer examination, might turn out to be different. The fact is, readers don't trust writers who sound vague, because the authors seem unsure of themselves.

Some words that indicate vague writing

Some words that are telltale signs of vague writing are:

sort of, thing, kind of, seem, approximately, about, appear,
look as if, roughly, more or less, give or take, almost,
nearly, apparently.

Example: The man was approximately ten feet away when he started screaming.

It does not make a difference to the reader whether the man was exactly ten feet or ten feet three inches away. You sound waffly when you write thus.

Instead, write:

(Corrected) The man was ten feet away when he started screaming.

(Vague) It looked like some sort of red sauce on what appeared to be a piece of bread.

(Corrected) There was tomato sauce on the rye bread.

Exercise—Vague writing

Recast the following sentences to be more assertive or clearer:

1. There was a kind of paste sticking to the brush.
2. It seemed to be a human skeleton with one of the leg bones missing.
3. The triangle was roughly 2.09876 square millimetre in area.
4. I think she was nearly forty-five minutes late for an interview.
5. The petrol tank was almost nearly full when we started out.
6. The adult population that supported the hypothesis was more or less 10.4%, give or take a percentage point or two.
7. I would argue that the ratio of males to females in this country is reducing.

Answers—Vague writing

1. There was toothpaste on the brush.
2. It was a human skeleton minus a femur.
3. The triangle was 2.09876 square millimetres in area.
4. She was forty-five minutes late for an interview.
5. The petrol tank was full when we started out.
6. 10.4% of the adult population supported the hypothesis.
7. The ratio of males to females in this country is reducing.

'Huh?' Sentences

These are words, phrases, or sentences that can make the reader go 'huh'. Use them advisedly and with awareness. They don't sound great in prose. In any case, don't use an unintended assonance, rhyme, or pun in your writing.

Assonance

Assonance is a literary device in which vowel sounds are repeated in words that are nearby within a sentence.

Avoid always awful assonances.

The assonance can be within a word, within a phrase, or within a sentence. It can sound wonderful in poetry.

Perfectly voiceless,
Widen the crannies,
Shoulder through holes. We...

SYLVIA PLATH, *MUSHROOMS*

The above has assonance in the 'o' of 'shoulder' and the 'o' of holes.

Alliteration

Alliteration is the repetition of the first consonant sound in neighbouring words. An example of alliteration is:

'Peter Piper prefers pickles.'

Alliterations and assonances often distract the reader and are best avoided in prose writing, unless done deliberately. In poetry, they can work wonderfully well.

The fair breeze blow, the white foam flew,

The furrow followed free

SAMUEL TAYLOR COLERIDGE, *RIME OF THE ANCIENT MARINER*

Rhymes

It is a good practice to watch out for unintended rhymes in prose writing.

'Take a hike,' said Mike.

Puns

Puns also grab attention, and you should avoid them, except in certain types of comic writing.

This is my stated position, but I am not above sneaking in a pun or two in comic writing. For instance, in the *Sorcerer of Mandala,* I confess, I have written the following lines:

As Kip Ling, the ancient Chinese philosopher, remarked, 'Yeast is yeast and vest is vest and never the twain shall meet. For you get starched underwear and plenty of discomfort.'

I once asked a publisher, 'What do you think of author branding?'

'Some authors deserve all they can get,' he replied, 'preferably with a hot iron rod.'

Authorial intrusions

One goal in writing is to create or describe worlds that are believable. Even if the events described therein are fantastic, the writer tries to ensure that she suspends the reader's disbelief for the time being. If the voice of the author intrudes in-between, it is hard to keep such a fiction going. It is analogous to breaking the fourth wall in a play.

Earlier, often, the author addressed the reader in the middle of the narrative.

And that, gentle reader, is how to set the golden fleas free.

Sometimes, the author sidetracked the narrative to seek the reader's opinion. As in:

What would you do in that position? Give up, or fight?

Here is an actual quote:

.... And here I have lamely related to you the uneventful chronicle of two foolish children in a flat who most unwisely sacrificed for each other the greatest treasures of their house. But in a last word to the wise of these days, let it be said that of all who give gifts these two were the wisest. O all who give and receive gifts, such as they are wisest. Everywhere they are wisest. They are the magi.

O'HENRY, *GIFT OF THE MAGI*

This is no longer passé. You must certainly avoid authorial intrusion if you are using a first- person or third-person limited POV.

Sentence fragments

A sentence needs a primary subject and a verb. When either is missing, the sentence is incomplete and is a sentence fragment.

Use sentence fragments in writing fiction, but only when necessary. Do not overuse them.

Short, choppy sentence fragments can give an urgent feel to the paragraph. Use them when you want to create that effect.

The following is a passage from *Songs of the Cauvery:*

Long expressive eyes. Plaited hair that reached her hips. A heady smell of jasmine.

'I have something important to tell you.'

A lift of an eyebrow. Jangle of earrings.

'You have to forget me. We cannot live together.'

Ellipses...

Please do not use ellipses indiscriminately, imagining that you are writing timeless stream-of-consciousness prose.

A smell in the air... a beautiful woman... trekking through the flowers... I thought of my skin condition....

Don't do it.

Wimpy prose

Waffling words are phrases, such as I believe, I think, perhaps, possibly, allegedly, it is reported that.

As an author, you should appear confident and trustworthy. If you use waffling words, the reader will be put off.

Euphemisms

Euphemisms exist for many things. For instance, they can be connected with:

- death
- looks of a person and body attributes
- sexual activities
- employment
- bodily functions
- ageing

Examples: chubby, plump, big, demise, passed away (died), let go (fired)

Of late, there are a number of euphemisms in marketing speak. Second-hand books, toys, and clothes all become 'pre-loved'; casualties and fatalities become 'collateral damage'; and fired becomes 'terminated'.

Dysphemisms

A dysphemism is a derogatory euphemism.

There are dysphemisms for:

- Death: There are more euphemisms for death than anything else—passed away, passed over to the other side, late, dearly departed, resting in peace, no longer with us, passed, gone to heaven, has gone to the great kennel in the sky, negative patient outcome.
- Lack of intelligence: not the sharpest knife in the drawer
- Smart people: egghead, bookworm
- Aged: geezer
- Occupation- based: shrink (for a psychiatrist), ambulance-chaser (for a lawyer), quack (for a doctor)

As far as possible, don't use euphemisms or dysphemisms.

Slang

Make sure that the slang used in the dialogue is appropriate for the era. Most dictionaries tell you the year of the first use of a word or phrase. You can also look it up in the Google Ngram viewer.

Most slang words, except for a handful like 'cool', come with a short expiry date. So, it is better to avoid using slang altogether in the narrative. One obvious disadvantage of using slang in your prose is that you, as an author, will be dated.

Unfortunate choice of words

Sometimes, your choice of words can lead to a comical or unfortunate linkage in the reader's mind. Hunt and destroy these. Examples include:

- He bent backwards to please his gymnastics coach.
- She tried to outwit the burglar but shot herself in the foot.
- He watched the heart-wrenching Aztec sacrifice from his hiding place.
- The archaeologist left no stone unturned in his search for the missing mummy.

Do the math

Please be aware that you could be using terms of statistics wrongly or causing mirth among the mathematicians who read it.

Here are two actual sentences I read:

- On an average, there were taller boys in the class.
- Billions of my readers will love this.

When you are quoting numbers, make sure that you are at least in the same order. If there were a thousand, don't say 'tens'. Don't refer to 'millions' as 'billions'. They differ by several orders.

The right register

The extent of formality in the writing depends on the type of writing and the era in which it is set.

For instance, the following are usually formal:

- business letters
- letters to and from government organisations
- legal communication
- academic writing

The following are often informal:

- personal emails
- personal messages

Neutral register

Many stories are in a neutral register. Some non-academic essays and letters can also be in a neutral tone.

Social register

In many situations, you might need to distinguish a social register. The language may reflect it either in your narrative or in dialogue. Avoid doing this in the narrative. Even in dialogue, while it is fine to distinguish different forms of speech (in terms of direct and slang used), it is not at all a good idea to mimic an accent.

Charles Dickens used dialogue to distinguish social registers. These are in the words of the incomparable Sam Weller:

> *'All good feelin', sir–the wery best intentions, as the gen'l'm'n said ven he run away from his wife 'cos she seemed unhappy with him.'*
>
> *'There; now we look compact and comfortable, as the father said ven he cut his little boy's head off, to cure him o' squintin'.'*
>
> CHARLES DICKENS, *PICKWICK PAPERS*

To reiterate, even though Dickens mimicked accents in his writing, it is now passé.

Using words ending in '-ing'

Sentences with words ending in '-ing' (I am not talking about words like king and bling) can be clunky and harder to understand.

Words ending in '-ing' can be gerunds, participles, or progressive verbs, or they can be used in an absolute phrase. (Don't panic. I will explain what these mean in a moment.) Exercise caution while using '-ing' words. Since these words can be used in multiple senses, they can end up confusing the reader. This often leads to their overuse, resulting in awkward unintended rhymes in your writing. They can also lead to errors of parallelism, ambiguity, complexity, and plain awkwardness.

Gerunds

Gerunds are nouns ending in '-ing' and they are made from verbs. For example:

Sitting, as a form of exercise, is underrated.

Here, 'sitting' is a gerund since it functions as a noun made from the verb 'sit'.

Problem with gerunds

Consider the following example:

(Complex) Engaging in banter with fellow-employees is a recipe for disaster.

This sentence slows down the reader while he tries to understand it.

(Simpler) If you engage in banter with fellow-employees, it can be disastrous.

Or,

(Simpler) It is disastrous to banter with fellow-employees.

Participles/progressive verb forms

Verbs and adjectives ending in '-ing' are participles. For example:

I was slobbering.

Here, 'slobbering' is in the participle form and is a verb. It is a present participle, to be precise.

'Slobbering' can also act as an adjective, as in:

The slobbering man was elected as President.

The '-ing' form that acts like a verb can slow down your writing. There is usually a more concise way to write it. 'He was slobbering' can simply be rewritten as 'he slobbered', unless you want to indicate the continuous nature of the action, as in:

He was still slobbering when they found him.

Progressive verbs are verbs showing that an action is ongoing. The issue with progressive verbs is that we use them one too often when a simple verb would suffice. Consider the following sentences:

He had been working late every day at the office.

He was working as his son knitted.

In the above sentences, use 'worked'. The meaning will not change too much.

He worked late every day at the office.

He worked as his son knitted.

Unintended concurrency

Sometimes, the participle can describe impossible-to-perform concurrent actions.

Singing, he popped the chocolates into his mouth.

This is a rather crude example. If you start your sentences with participles often enough, you will encounter such problems, sometimes, far subtler than this.

(Recast) He stopped singing long enough to pop the chocolates into his mouth.

Consider another example:

Running along the forest path, she peeked behind every tree.

I dare say it is difficult to do the running and peeking concurrently. This can be recast as:

Running along the forest path, she stopped now and then to peek behind a tree.

Stative verbs

These are verbs indicative of state rather than an action. Examples include verbs of thought like know, understand, like, believe; verbs of feeling like fear, love; and verbs of possession like have, own.

You cannot form past or present continuous tense with stative verbs. So, you cannot use the '-ing' form of these verbs to indicate a continuous sense.

(Incorrect) I was fearing this would happen.

(Revised) I feared this would happen.

Absolute phrases

Rain pouring down ceaselessly, the cricket match was abandoned.

Such construction is great for poetry, but sometimes, plain is better, as in:

(Recast) Since the rain poured down ceaselessly, the cricket match was abandoned.

The other issue with the use of absolute phrases can be seen in the following example:

The rain pouring down ceaselessly, she completed her homework.

The absolute phrase in the sentence (The rain pouring down ceaselessly) has nothing to do with the rest of the sentence and has been used as a glue for pasting two sentences together. Avoid such usage. Do not overuse such constructions involving absolute phrases.

Other issues with '-ing' words

Dangling the modifiers

Consider the following sentences:

1. Going in to bat first, the pitch was pacy.
2. Heckling the speaker on the podium, the speaker was very nervous..
3. Knowing that the match was a crucial one, Sachin's feet moved in complex ways.

Notice that in the above sentences, the preceding phrase (before the first comma) attempts to modify something but is left dangling because it has nothing to change. The corrected sentences are:

1. Going into bat first, he found the pitch pacy. (The pitch did not go in to bat.)
2. Heckling the speaker on the podium, she made the speaker nervous. (Surely, the speaker did not heckle himself.)
3. Knowing that the match was a crucial one, Sachin moved his feet in complex ways. (Sachin's feet did not have the knowledge.)

Stringing together too many actions

> Speeding through the traffic, Ganesh kept swearing. His wife, trying to pacify him, waving her hands about, trying to calm him down, failed utterly.

To bring some balance to the above passage, you can try:

> As Ganesh sped through the traffic, he swore. His wife, trying to pacify him, waved her hands about but failed to calm him.

Use '-ing' words, but know the pitfalls of doing so.

PART 4:

WORDS, WORDS!

Chapter 10
Complex Words

Rule 10: Develop Your Unique Voice

Simple vs. complex words

Use a simple word rather than a long-winded one. Don't be sesquipedalian. I am not suggesting you be hippopotomonstrosesquipedaliophobic either. I am only asking you not to use long words habitually. Just don't fear long words, and use them occasionally.

If you are like me, it might help you to run away after you call someone (like Winston Churchill did) a 'purveyor of terminological inexactitudes'. Scamper away before your opponent realises that you just called him a liar. Here is one form of the sentence that is attributed to Dr Samuel Johnson:

> *Allow me to dip the extremities of my digits into the receptacle of yours, which contains a pulverised substance which, when thrust into the olfactory organ, produces a tingling and scintillating sensation.*

He asked for snuff.

Don't be like Johnson or like Churchill.

Caveat (oops, I mean warning):

> *Make everything as simple as possible, but not simpler.*
>
> Albert Einstein

Don't use very short words and sentences repeatedly. Instead, vary their length. You may not want to sound like Dr Seuss on amphetamines.

No two words in the English language are identical in the precise shade of their meaning. I am exaggerating but only a little. For instance, look at some synonyms of the word 'pain':

Suffering—Pain is the cause and suffering, the result. They are not identical.

Agony—Agony is suffering dialled-up.

Ache—An ache is localised in a particular part of the body, whereas pain is more generalised.

Torment—It is a repeated pain that is caused by someone or something.

Still, I advise you to choose a simpler word when possible, but don't be afraid to use a long word if that gives you the exact nuance desired.

Alternative synonyms

Write 'use' instead of 'utilise' and 'read' instead of 'peruse'. 'Ask' rather than 'enquire', 'start' rather than 'commence'.

If you must use an unusual word, don't repeat it in its vicinity in the text. If it is a very complex word, don't use it elsewhere in the book. Better still, do not use it even in any of your other works.

See Appendix 4 for a few simpler replacements for more complex words.

Exercise—Complex words

Rewrite the following sentences using simpler words where warranted:

1. Anyone who wants to rent the unoccupied premises can contact the undersigned.
2. It appeared as though the very skies had opened up.
3. It is this very fact I was talking about.
4. There are a number of things that can go wide off the mark.
5. It is an entirely viable, workable solution to your problem.
6. Can you validate by the end of the day as to whether it warrants wasting further time on it?
7. Whereas the adult dragon was bald, the young one was furry.
8. I wanted to talk to you with reference to your compensation.
9. I witnessed an old man successfully negotiate a street crossing.
10. I am arresting you under the provisions of the Pugnacious Police Officers Act.
11. Until such time as you repent, you are grounded.
12. My office posted me to Assam. Subsequently, I had to relocate to Paris.
13. Provided that you study hard, you will pass the examination.
14. It may be advantageous to transmit the letter by post.
15. In as much as they wanted to live in close proximity to Tom's school, they shifted residence.

Answers—Complex words

1. Anyone who wants to rent the vacant place may contact me.
   Or,
   To rent the vacant place, contact me.
2. It looked like the skies had opened up.
3. I am talking about this.
   Or,
   This is what I am talking about.
4. Many things can go wrong.
5. It's practical.
6. Tell me today if we need to spend more time on this.
7. The adult dragon was bald, but the young one was furry.
8. I wanted to talk to you about your salary.
9. I saw an old man crossing the road.
10. I am arresting you under the Pugnacious Police Officers Act.
11. You are grounded till you repent.
12. My office posted me to Assam. Later, I had to move to Paris.
13. If you study hard, you will pass the examination.
14. The letter should be sent by post.
    Or, better still,
    Post the letter.
15. Since they wanted to live near Tom's school, they moved.

Foreign words

There are some extremely descriptive words in languages other than English, too. It is better to wait for them to be more commonly used in English before you use them yourself. For instance, you may be fascinated by the phrase *innerer Schweinehund* (inner pig-dog) in German that refers to an inner voice that says 'don't get up as yet'. Don't use such words.

Some Latin words like 'carpe diem' or 'sine qua non', etc. are, however, fair game, and you may use them boldly (though not in boldface) in all their unitalicised glory. There are some more words that you can use, but we will discuss them later.

Some unemphasised foreign words

Don't italicise foreign words that have long been used in English. The ultimate determiner is the style guide you or the publication follow. Some of the foreign words that are used without emphasis are:

Déjà vu (French)—It refers to a feeling that you have already experienced the present situation.

Etc. (Latin)—It is the short form of et cetera. It means 'and so on' or 'things of a similar kind'.

Et al. (Latin)—It means 'and others'. Use it when the names of people are left out.

Ibid. (Latin)—It is the short form of ibidem, which means 'from the same place'. It refers to the same source as the previous one.

A priori (Latin)—It refers to something that follows from a self-evident proposition.

Faux pas (French)—It refers to an embarrassing mistake.

Ex ante (Latin)—It refers to something that is subjective and based on assumptions and estimates.

Pièce de résistance (French)—It is the showpiece among various objects, often used in connection with a meal.

Schadenfreude (German)—It is the pleasure that you get from someone else's misfortune.

Nom de guerre (French)—This is an assumed name or a pseudonym.

Non sequitur (Latin)—It refers to a statement that does not logically follow from the previous one.

Nouveau riche (French)—It means 'the newly rich'.

Objet d'art (French)—It refers to a small artistic object.

Words of a particular culture

In writing about a culture where English is not spoken, you encounter another problem—whether or not to translate words that are unique to the culture.

I ran into a similar problem while writing *Songs of the Cauvery*. I wrote the book from an insider's point of view rather than describing events in a touristy way.

Some terms were not easily translatable. They would have required multiple paragraphs to explain. I did not want to replace them with other English words that were roughly equivalent, as it would have made my writing look inauthentic. I also did not want to add lengthy footnotes, since this would have taken the attention away from the narrative.

I used the original words in Sanskrit or Tamil but made sure that I used the words in such a way that:

- Not understanding the word did not affect the reader's grasp of the story.
- The context gave a rough understanding of the word.
- It was possible to google each of those words.

Here is an example from *Songs of the Cauvery* where all three conditions are fulfilled in the use of the word 'janavasam'.

The janavasam—the procession of the bridegroom—was conducted with Panju sitting in…

Redundant words

We often repeat the patterns of our speech in writing, forgetting that there is much more time to think while writing. Sometimes, when we speak, we are at a loss for words. We use filler words, such as 'really' and 'like'. Often, we are stymied for words, and we substitute a weaselly general-purpose word.

There is no need to carry such practices into our writing. Even if you use such words while writing the first draft, it is worthwhile to hunt down and replace such words during an editing pass, making your text crisper.

Examples of filler words include:

really, actually, just, completely, entirely, truly, obviously, clearly, undoubtedly

For further examples, see Appendix 4.

For instance, instead of 'There was actually a problem', write, 'There was a problem.'

Exercise—Redundant words

Change the following sentences by using a simple word instead of the more complex one. Remove the redundant word.

1. It was really a brilliant show.
2. By the time I thought I had completed the exercise totally, the teacher gave another.

3. Let this be a caveat to all clear-thinking individuals — do not repeat this again.
4. It was becoming abundantly clear that the solution to the problems commences with ourselves.
5. I was alone by myself, when it struck me that I should eschew the sesquipedalian.
6. Inhabitants of vitreous tenements shouldn't launch lithic missiles.
7. He was truly the archetypical moron.
8. Her evasive circumlocution truly exasperated me.
9. How do I love thee? Let me enumerate the possibilities.
10. I felt insulted. It was a bit of a Backpfeifengesicht for me.

Answers—Redundant words

1. It was a brilliant show.
2. By the time I thought I had completed the exercise, the teacher gave another.
3. Let this be a warning to all clear-thinking individuals — do not repeat this.
4. The solution to the problems begins with us.
5. I was by myself, when it struck me that I shouldn't use long words.
6. People in glass houses shouldn't throw stones.
7. He was a typical moron.
8. Her evasion annoyed me.
9. How do I love thee? Let me count the ways.
10. I felt insulted. It was a bit of a slap in the face.

Distancing the Reader

Filter words

Filter words increase the distance between you (the writer) and the reader. You lose the reader's involvement. The reader loses his emotional investment in the piece of work because of the psychological distance created.

If you are in the point of view of a character, you are seeing through her eyes, hearing through her ears, and sensing the external world through her senses. Hence, there is no need to write 'she saw', 'she heard', or 'she smelt'.

'Saw', 'heard', and 'smelt' are filter words.

(Original) She saw the hunter approach her.

(Revised) The hunter approached.

(Original) David saw that the water was dripping from the leaves.

(Revised) Water dripped from the leaves.

Clearly, the revised versions are more direct, immediate, and concise. In the second revised version, assuming that the author writes from the point of view of David, there is no loss of information.

A progressive distancing

In the following example, each sentence takes the reader further away:

- The bandit approached.
- She saw the bandit approach.
- She could see the bandit approach.
- She thought he could see the bandit approach.

You only think you see the reader nearby but you don't. He is away and running.

Here is a list of a few filter words you can check for in your writing:

Sense words

saw, observed, noticed, spotted, heard, smelt, felt

Mental state words

realised, decided

Emotional state words

wondered, saddened

When to use sense words

There is nothing wrong with the filter words themselves. Just use them with care. You could certainly use them:

- When you are establishing POV at the beginning of a section of narrative. For instance:

David saw the waterfall and was astounded. The water poured in a ceaseless torrent...

- When you are switching the POV. For instance, assume that so far, the narration has been in David's point of view. You switch to Esther's POV (Don't switch in the middle of a scene.):

David was getting tired. Esther, however, was not. She saw the water dripping from the leaves and knew there was something wrong.

- When you want to stay with the actor and don't want to break up the action. For instance:

Even before David entered the room, he smelt cordite.

- When you need to give importance to the sensing. For instance:

David smelt blood. He dropped to his haunches and licked the red splotch.

- When it is critical to the meaning in the narrative. For instance, imagine your POV character dies (violently or otherwise) mid-scene. You will need to shift the POV to describe the body (add other gory bits here).

To fix the filter word, make sure you are in the right POV. Simply remove the sense words and recast the sentence.

(Original) She saw the man approach.

(Recast) The man approached.

Words of emotional state

These include verbs denoting an emotional state, such as wondered, rued. These can be static and inactive.

(Original) How could this be solved, he wondered.

(Recast) *How do I solve this?*

(Note the italics, implying thought. Very often, you can even do away with the italics.)

Words of mental state

Verbs such as decided, knew, thought, believed, and realised make the narrative wordy.

To fix these, drop the word and imply that this is the thought of the POV character.

(Original) He saw the pink lion. He believed that he was going crazy.

(Revised) He saw the pink lion. *I am going crazy.*

Exercise—Words of sense, thought, and emotion

Recast the following sentences:

1. He noticed the lion licking its lips.
2. She observed the fly on his nose.
3. He heard the loud sound that felt bizarre amidst the desert.
4. He felt uneasy.
5. He wondered how it would be if he were to abandon the search at that point.
6. She believed that she could see the entire world from the top of the 100-storey building.
7. He realised with a shudder that what he felt was the raspy tongue of a Gila monster.
8. He thought he could see a lion at a distance.

Answers—Words of sense, thought, and emotion

1. The lion licked its lips.
2. A fly had settled on his nose.
3. The loud sound was bizarre. (Note that both the hearing and feeling are gone. Assuming that you have already placed the protagonist in the desert, there is no need for repetition.)
4. He tensed.
5. *Should I abandon the search now?*
6. She saw the entire world from the top of the 100-storey building.
7. The raspy tongue of a Gila monster brushed against his hand.
8. *Was that a lion?*

Vague Words

Rather than use filter words and other vague words, use words that are direct and specific. Vague and non-specific words take away the reader's attention. They leave the reader with no clear image to latch on to.

Replace intensifiers, such as 'very', with stronger, more specific words.

(Original) She walked very fast.

(Revised) She walked rapidly.

(Original) He was very tired.

(Revised) He was exhausted.

See Appendix 5 for some 'very' words and possible alternatives.

Exercise—Vague modifiers

Use appropriate verbs instead of intensifiers in the sentences given below. Use a reverse dictionary if needed.

1. She felt very afraid and very cold.
2. He wore a very clear bathrobe that showed off his anatomy in intimate detail.
3. The odds of such a thing happening were vanishingly low.
4. He was extremely biased in his views and always stuck to what he believed in.
5. He was very curious.
6. The exceedingly low levels to which he could sink were clear from this.
7. She had a very confident demeanour.
8. It was a very difficult situation in which he found himself.
9. She was very surprised.
10. He was very concerned that his son would get into the wrong company.
11. He stared at the extremely deformed branch of a tree.
12. How dare she do this? He was very angry.
13. Sheila very consciously led Ashok to believe that she was telling the truth.
14. Why does Kensington act like this? Barbara was very confused.
15. She had to pay the examination fee by the next day. She was getting very desperate.
16. Some very enthusiastic followers of the leader had blocked the road.
17. She was very set on appearing very confident at the interview.
18. This is a very dangerous mission. It could cost you your life.
19. This is a very difficult puzzle to solve.
20. 'I think,' the speaker concluded, 'this is a very equitable plan for all concerned.'

Answers—Vague modifiers

1. She was freezing and frightened.
2. He wore a transparent bathrobe that showed off his anatomy in intimate detail.
3. The probability of that happening was infinitesimal.
4. He was opinionated.

5. He was inquisitive.
6. The abysmal levels to which he could sink were clear from this.
7. She was poised.
8. He was in a crisis.
9. She was astounded.
10. He was worried that his son would get into the wrong company.
11. He stared at the twisted branch of a tree.
12. How dare she do this? He was furious.
13. Sheila deliberately led Ashok to believe that she was telling the truth.
14. Why does Kensington act like this? Barbara was baffled.
15. She had to pay the examination fee by the next day. She was frantic.
16. Some over-zealous followers of the leader had blocked the road.
17. She was determined to be poised at the interview.
18. This is a perilous mission. It could cost you your life.
19. This is a complicated puzzle.
20. 'I think,' the speaker concluded, 'this is a fair plan.'

Other imprecise words

You should prefer the specific to the general, the concrete to the vague—words such as thing, sort of, kind of, a lot, and used.

Particularly in technical writing, the word 'use' is unacceptable. It allows for vague, imprecise, and incomplete descriptions.

(Original) You can navigate to any part of the screen using the command and the arrow keys.

(Revised) To go up, press the command key and the up-arrow key simultaneously.

(Original) I wore that thing that one wears on the thumb to prevent getting pricked by the needle.

(Revised) I wore a thimble.

(Original) There is a kind of people who shouldn't be throwing stones.

(Revised) People in glass houses shouldn't throw stones.

'Some' words

It is worth examining words starting with 'some', such as something, somewhere, somehow, sometimes, and somebody. You may be able to replace them with words that convey your meaning more accurately.

Fix: Replace 'sometimes' with specific times, 'something' with the specific thing and so on.

(Original) Sometimes, time seems to fly.

(Fixed) When you are having fun, time seems to fly.

(Original) Somehow, I escaped the guillotine.

(Fixed) I had previously dug a tunnel underneath for just this sort of emergency. I simply jumped into it and escaped the guillotine.

Exercise—Vague words

Change the vague word in the following sentences into one more specific or precise:

1. He managed to kill the vampire somehow.
2. Someone had filled the wall with graffiti.
3. He was somewhat frayed by the time he made the journey.
4. Someone else is in your arms tonight.
5. He travelled a lot.
6. That was a big statue.
7. It was a good diamond.
8. You must learn to accept bad situations in life.

Answers—Vague words

1. Having applied the garlic paste to the pointed stick he had prepared before, he drove the stake with a mallet into the vampire's heart, killing it instantly.
2. The young boy took out a spray can of mauve paint from his trousers. He sprayed with quick hands and drew with clean lines. As soon as Tom said, 'Hey, what are you doing?' the boy abandoned the graffiti, rushed to his motorcycle and rode off.
3. His clothes were torn, his hair dishevelled, and his face was streaked with dirt by the time he completed his journey.
4. I knew it. That backstabbing, double-dealing smooth operator Ken. You are dancing with him tonight, aren't you?
5. He travelled every week.
6. It was a colossal statue of Chatrapati Shivaji.

7. It was a flawless diamond.
8. You must learn to accept adverse situations in life.

Adverbs and Adjectives

You might have often heard the writing advice—'avoid adverbs'. The primary rationale for this advice is that adverbs (and adjectives) promote telling rather than showing.

What is an adverb?

An adverb is a modifier. Usually, adverbs modify verbs. They can also modify adjectives, other adverbs, phrases, and even entire sentences. Examples include 'walked quickly', 'said abruptly'.

Here, 'quickly' and 'abruptly' are adverbs that modify the verbs 'walked' and 'said'.

Adverbs can be of different types. Not all of them deserve to be looked at with suspicion.

Types of adverbs

Adverbs can be of one of the following types:

- Conjunctive adverbs: however, nevertheless, meanwhile
- Adverbs of frequency: often, oftentimes, usually, never, sometimes
- Adverbs of time: yesterday, today, tomorrow, eventually
- Adverbs of place: here, nowhere, there, inside, outside
- Adverbs of degree: really, barely
- Adverbs of manner: quickly, rapidly, slowly, angrily

Adverbs of manner

The advice, 'avoid adverbs', is mainly to be applied to adverbs of manner and adverbs of degree.

Adverbs of manner answer the question 'how'—in what manner the action (represented by the modified verb) takes place. Typical examples of such adverbs are adjectives converted into adverbs by adding '-ly'. For example, quickly, rapidly, slowly, and angrily.

There are a few problems with adverbs of manner.

Adverbs of manner promote telling over showing. This can bore your reader. Adverbs are particularly insidious when they are a part of the dialogue tag, as in:

(Original) 'Why don't you come in for a nightcap?' she asked, flirtatiously.

The dialogue itself shows the intention, and the adverb needlessly describes it. If the lily needed gilding, you could have said something like:

(Revised) 'Why don't you come in for a nightcap?' she asked, mussing my hair.

Strong verbs are often better than adverbs

(Original) She walked quickly to the store.
(Revised) She rushed to the store.

(Original) He walked quickly to the bus stop.
(Revised) He sprinted to the bus stop.

(Original) The cat walked quickly across the room.
(Revised) The cat scampered across the room.

(Original) The car drove quickly down the road.
(Revised) The car zoomed down the road.

(Original) The jogger walked quickly around the park.
(Revised) The jogger pounded the pavement around the park.

For more examples, see Appendix 6.

By using an adverb, you might lose some understated elegance. It is a good practice for authors to let the readers connect the dots. Adverbs often add an unneeded description, spoiling the effect for the intelligent reader.

'Next time, you should be more careful in class,' I said.
'Whatever,' she said, uninterestedly.

Adverbs of degree

Some adverbs of degree introduce redundancy and can even convey the opposite meaning.

For example, consider 'He is truly honest.' 'He is honest' is good enough. Not only is it 'truly' superfluous, it also calls the truthfulness of the narrator into question. The reader wonders, 'Is he really honest?'

When to use adverbs

While using adverbs of manner, make sure that no stronger verb exists or there is no clearer way of showing.

Sometimes, adverbs can be a cleaner and shorter way to depict something.

(Original) He continued to behave in an unthinking manner.

(Revised) He continued to behave thoughtlessly.

Exercise—Eliminating adverbs

Recast the following sentences using a stronger verb instead of the verb-adverb combination:

1. She spoke quietly.
2. He walked slowly towards her.
3. The children laughed loudly at the clown's antics.
4. The dog barked loudly and plaintively.
5. She cried softly.
6. He shouted loudly at the dog.
7. The water flowed slowly out of the barrel.
8. The wind blew strongly.
9. When she noticed Peter in the distance, she walked quickly to him.
10. When he saw the police officer coming, he ran away really fast.
11. She was very sad when her dog died.
12. On nearing the traffic lights, the driver drove really fast.
13. He looked menacingly at the champion.
14. Kim secretly listened to all her mother's conversations.
15. She walked shakily.
16. The zamindar treated the labourers very badly.
17. After an hour of exercise, he was exceedingly tired.
18. The sauce was mildly flavoured.

Answers—Eliminating adverbs

1. She whispered.
2. He sauntered towards her.
3. The children cackled at the clown's antics.
4. The dog yelped.
5. She sobbed.
6. He bellowed at the dog.
7. The water trickled out of the barrel.
8. The wind gusted.

9. When she noticed Peter in the distance, she rushed to him.
10. When he saw the police officer coming, he scooted.
11. She was miserable when her dog died.
12. On nearing the traffic lights, the driver speeded.
13. He glared at the champion.
14. Kim eavesdropped on all her mother's conversations.
15. She tottered.
16. The zamindar oppressed the labourers.
17. After an hour of exercise, he was exhausted.
18. The sauce was bland.

Adjectives

Like adverbs, adjectives are modifiers. Usually, adjectives qualify/modify nouns.

Examples: small car, big house, beautiful face, crooked nose

Here, 'small', 'big', 'beautiful', and 'crooked' are adjectives that modify various nouns.

Adjectives to watch out for

Redundant adjectives

Redundant adjectives are adjectives that are not really necessary. Oops! I mean, adjectives that are not necessary.

Example: A really big mansion

The noun 'mansion' is descriptive enough—'a mansion' would do.

'Nothing' adjectives

You can omit these adjectives with no change in the meaning.

Example: exact same, freshly rejuvenated.

Often-used, almost-clichéd, or vague adjectives

These are adjectives that we have seen so often that they don't trigger any images in our minds.

Example: happy, sad, bad, nice, big

Why not try: grief-stricken, miserable, corrupt, infamous, notorious, satisfying, gratifying, delicate, humongous, gargantuan, etc.?

Adjectives that tell

These are adjectives that imply a value-based judgement. Adjectives that are based on evidence are fine, but take a second look at those that stem from your prejudice or your knowledge outside of what you have written.

For instance, 'he was a corrupt man.' Here, 'corrupt' may be a value-based judgement on your part. If you had shown sufficient evidence, then this would have been acceptable. But then again, if you have shown sufficient evidence, it is better to let the reader infer than forcing a value-based judgement.

On the other hand, using an adjective is a shortcut where you don't want to use all those words, while showing.

Adjective-on-adjective

Don't use too many adjectives modifying the same noun. Choose one.

Example: He wore a hard, mean look.

'He wore a mean look' is adequate.

Exercise—Adjectives

Tighten the following sentences:

1. It was a very spacious palace.
2. He was a tall giant at over seven feet.
3. It was an unnecessary pleonasm.
4. He was good at communicating his meaningful ideas.
5. The sentence is redundantly superfluous.
6. She felt sad thinking of all the old days.
7. The brave superhero bowed deeply with a flourish of the cape.
8. 'Verdant green' is an overused cliché.
9. The institution was originally founded by Jawaharlal Nehru.
10. Look who is here. An unexpected surprise.

Answers—Adjectives

Explanations are given within brackets.

1. It was a palace. (All palaces are spacious.)
2. He was a giant at over seven feet. (Or better still, 'He was over seven feet.' There is no need to distinguish between a tall giant and a medium-sized one.)
3. It was a pleonasm. (Pleonasm is the use of more words than necessary.)
4. He was good at communicating his ideas. (All ideas are meaningful.)
5. The sentence is superfluous. (Redundant means superfluous.)
6. She felt melancholic.

7. The superhero bowed deeply, with a flourish of the cape.
8. 'Verdant green' is a cliché. (Of course, verdant means green and, therefore, is superfluous.)
9. The institution was founded by Jawaharlal Nehru. ('Originally' is superfluous.)
10. Look who is here. A surprise! (All surprises are unexpected.)

Words that Bore

When you have seen a word again and again, you get annoyed if you see it one more time. Words such as 'go' and 'get' belong to this category. They are also overloaded words (meaning, words that have multiple meanings).

Words like got, go, put, ate, look, walk, run, sit, stand, and keep can be boring, and an alternative can carry far more information.

Consider the following words and how they come to life when you use a more descriptive verb:

Instead of 'He walked', you can say, 'He ambled/sauntered/plodded/staggered.'

Each of the above alternatives adds a nuance to the meaning.

Similarly:

went > reached, proceeded, advanced, retired, drove, cycled, flew

put > placed, set, positioned, propped, leaned, arranged, lay

sit > perch, flop

Look up a thesaurus. One of the words may communicate the exact meaning that you intend conveying.

Exercise—Boring words

Change the word/words in italics in the sentences below:

1. The bird *sat* on the high wire.
2. She *walked fast*, lest she should miss the appointment.
3. She *put* the figurine next to the desk lamp on the table.
4. He *ate* his food *in a hurry*.
5. The child *stood still* on hearing the sudden noise.
6. *Keep* the mobile phone in your hand on the ground, and raise your hands.
7. Exhausted, he *sat* on the sofa with the comfortable cushions.

8. *Every time* I *go* to him for a raise, he says a performance appraisal is due.
9. The ploughman, *towards his home, walks with a heavy stride* on his weary way.

Answers—Boring words

1. The bird *perched* on the high wire.
2. She *hurried,* lest she should miss the appointment.
3. She *positioned* the figurine next to the desk lamp on the table.
4. He *bolted* down his food.
5. The child *froze* on hearing the sudden noise.
6. *Place* the mobile phone in your hand on the ground, and raise your hands.
7. Exhausted, he *flopped* on the sofa with the comfortable cushions.
8. Whenever I *approach* him for a raise, he says a performance appraisal is due.
9. The ploughman homeward *plods* his weary way.

Clichés

Times, they are a-changin', surely. When I was young, my father used to tell me to read the newspaper leader (editorial) and to note the idiomatic use of words. He exhorted me to write like that. Thank God, I never heeded that piece of advice. If I did that today, what I write would be castigated as cliché-ridden.

Clichéd sayings and phrases

Some clichés to avoid like the plague are:

- low-hanging fruit
- at the end of the day
- bite the bullet
- the cat's out of the bag
- the ball is in your court
- raining cats and dogs
- it's not rocket science
- easy as pie
- the pot calling the kettle black
- money doesn't grow on trees

Collocations

Collocations are words that often go together. For instance, 'excruciating' and 'pain' go together.

Some collocations are clichéd. Avoid them. You could do something more annoying by pairing a normally collocated word incorrectly. For instance, one 'commits' suicide, not 'indulges in' or 'organises', etc.

Fresh language vs. collocated words

Some collocations sound clichéd, but when you use a fresh verb or noun instead, it may sound strange. Just 'tread carefully' (not walk, step, tiptoe, saunter, or march). Over time, some collocations become clichéd, and others become a part of the shaded meaning of the word. For instance, you are welcome to tread where angels dare, tread on my toes, tread softly but not tread along a catwalk. If you want to, you are welcome to 'sashay'.

A lion might roar, and not howl or bellow (unless it is in pain) or cry out or shout.

When in doubt, use neither the word nor the collocation.

Clichéd adverbs/adjectives

Avoid adverbs and adjectives that do not add to the elements that modify. If you tell me one more time that man is a social animal, I am not responsible for what I will do.

Avoid making a striking contrast, feeling unbounded joy or true love. Don't be a rookie beginner. Nothing is absolutely necessary. Don't be utterly devastated.

Avoid adverbs and adjectives that are very often used. No 'suddenly' or 'awesome', please. Avoid, for instance:

I was enjoying my sandwiches when my mother called me suddenly.

There are also clichéd situations and storylines that you need to avoid, but that is a story for another day.

Exercise—Clichés

Figure out the clichés in the following sentences and fix them. Some have multiple awkward clichés :

1. If you play your cards right, you can make a killing in the poultry market.
2. He appears gentle as a mouse, but you cannot judge a book from its cover.

3. Once you have got the low hanging fruit, you can try for the main treasure.
4. Does it give you a buzz to act like this? Get rid of the bee in your bonnet.
5. If he loses this bet, that will be another nail in his coffin.
6. I will not accept his offer for a job. I don't want to be second best. He's the big cheese. I'll find other fish to fry.
7. He was armed to the teeth but survived the ambush by the skin of his teeth.
8. To cut a long story short, when are you finishing your epic multi-generational thriller?
9. Let's close ranks and come hell or high water, come up trumps.
10. Suddenly, he heard a sound that made him freeze.

Answers—Clichés

1. If you do the right things, you will make a huge profit in the poultry market.
2. He appears gentle. Don't be taken in by his appearance.
3. Once you complete the simple tasks, you can try to attain your primary goal.
4. Are you getting over-excited? Get rid of the thought.
5. If he loses his bet, he will be in a lot of trouble.
6. I will not accept his offer of a job. I don't want to be second best. He's the most important person. I'll find some other job.
7. He was fully armed but just managed to survive the ambush.
8. Let me get to the point. When are you finishing your epic multi-generational thriller?
9. Let us support each other and win.
10. He froze at the sound.

Chapter 11
Offensive Words

Some words offend a group of people by painting them or a group they are emotionally invested in, in a poor light or by misrepresenting them. What has the potential to offend keeps shifting. You will have to be clued in on what is currently happening in the world, and use appropriate words. The treatment of the subject here, therefore, is short.

Words of gender

There is a trend towards greater use of gender-neutral terms. Replace 'chairman' by 'chairperson' or simply the 'Chair'.

Similarly, 'sportsman', 'postman', 'fireman', 'saleswoman' are all passé.

Use 'flight attendant' instead of 'steward' or 'stewardess'.

Earlier, 'actor' meant male actor. 'Actress' was used for a female actor but not anymore. The term 'actor' is used for both.

Some politically incorrect words

Gendered

Man-made —> artificial
Forefathers —> ancestors
Salesman, saleswoman —> salesperson

Racist

Words of race, like Caucasian, Negro, and Mongoloid, are no longer in use.

The term 'people of colour' was earlier used for a 'non-white' population. BIPOC, the acronym, which stands for Black, Indigenous, and People of Colour, has gained popularity as a more inclusive term than 'people of colour' when talking about marginalised groups affected by racism.

Here are some recommendations:

Blackmail —> extort

Blacklisted—> banned
Eskimo —> inuit

Handicap

Deaf —> hearing impaired

Blind —> vision impaired

Religious

Christian name —> first name

Politically incorrect phrases

Sold down the river

When slavery was prevalent in the US, slave-owners in the North often sent their intractable slaves down the Mississippi River to a harder life in plantations in the Mississippi.

Cakewalk

'Cakewalk' is a word commonly used to describe a task that is extremely easy to perform. However, the word has 'dark' antecedents. There was a dance called 'The cakewalk', performed by slaves, before the Civil War. The winner of the contest received a cake. Worse still, the dance was also performed during slave auctions.

Master bedroom

This is a Dutch architectural term with colonial origins.

Foul language

Avoid use of foul language in academic writing and in writing meant for children.

In fiction writing, particularly in dialogue, if you want to keep in character, don't dumb down the intensity.

Don't use 'fricking' and other substitutes.

Don't even think of using '#$%^7' or its equivalent.

Use foul language in dialogue, if relevant, but eschew it in the narrative.

* * *

Petting the peeve

What is the point of writing a book if you cannot say what you want to say and cannot air your pet peeves? So, here goes. I have included a set of words and their usages that offend my ear and my sensibilities.

Cliché vs. clichéd

A cliché is a word, phrase, or expression that has lost its sheen with repeated usage. 'Cliché' is the noun form, and 'clichéd' is the adjective form. A well-worn expression is a cliché. It is not a cliché expression. It is a clichéd expression.

I am afraid it has gained currency through repeated wrong usage.

(Wrong) Don't say 'I beg to differ'. It's such a cliché expression.

(Corrected) Don't say 'I beg to differ'. It's such a clichéd expression.

(Correct) That's a cliché.

Enormity

'Enormity' does not show physical size. You may be amazed at the enormity of a crime, not at the perpetrator. If you must indicate physical size, use 'enormousness'.

(Wrong) The enormity of the giant stupefied me.

(Corrected) The enormousness of the giant stupefied me.

(Correct) The enormity of the mistake became clearer only after the radiation levels started increasing.

Grow

Don't use 'grow' transitively (meaning, grow something) unless you are growing tomatoes. Don't 'grow' your business. Grow up.

Literally

I am literally sick with people using 'literally' to mean nearly or metaphorically. If you literally die, you don't live to tell tales.

Nauseous

I think you should avoid using this word. You cannot get nauseous (well, you can, for instance, in situations involving you and a cannibal, but let me not confuse the issue). You get nauseated. 'Nauseous' is something that causes nausea. 'Nauseated' is to be affected with nausea. In fact, you can do away with the word entirely. Where you would use 'nauseous', use 'nauseating'.

(Wrong) When I smell coffee, I am nauseous.

(Corrected) When I smell coffee, I am nauseated.

(Correct) The coffee was nauseous.

(Correct) The coffee was nauseating.

Principle

More and more, I find 'principle' used where 'principal' ought to be used. It should be 'principal aims' not 'principle aims'. I had a school 'principal', not a 'principle'. I wonder whether it is too late. Has the usage already become mainstream?

'Principal', in its adjectival form, means 'main'. In the noun form, it can denote the main office-bearers of an organisation. 'Principle' is a basic rule or idea.

(Wrong) The principle element in air is nitrogen.

(Corrected) The principal element in air is nitrogen.

(Correct) The principles of organic farming are easy to grasp..

(Correct) Interest is payable quarterly on the principal.

(Correct) The principals of the firm were in Calcutta.

Preplan

'Preplan' literally means 'to plan beforehand'. How else do you plan? After the event? I think 'pre' here is as useful as an ingrown toenail. Just plan. Don't preplan.

(Wrong) I have to preplan my presentation carefully.

(Correct) I have to plan my presentation carefully.

Peruse

'Peruse' normally means to 'read carefully'. It has also come to mean the opposite — 'to read in a casual and superficial way'. So, I have stopped using the word altogether. I might use it sometime to show diplomatic doublespeak, as in:

'We have submitted the detailed documents to support our demands,' said the leader of the delegation.

'Ah,' said the duke, 'I shall certainly peruse it.'

Catch-22

A Catch-22 situation is a very specific kind of a paradoxical situation that takes its name from Joseph Keller's eponymous book.

> *There was only one catch, and that was Catch-22, which specified that a concern for one's own safety in the face of dangers that were real and immediate was the process of a rational mind. Orr was crazy and could be grounded. All he had to do was ask; and as soon as he did, he would no longer be crazy and would have to fly more missions. Orr would be crazy to fly more missions and sane if he didn't, but if he was sane, he had to fly them. If he flew them, he was crazy and didn't have to; but if he didn't want to, he was sane and had to. Yossarian was moved very deeply by the absolute simplicity of this clause of Catch-22 and let out a respectful whistle.*
>
> JOSEPH KELLER, *CATCH-22*

Just refer to any situation that is not a true Catch-22 as, simply, a 'catch'. Else, you will incur my perpetual wrath.

Chapter 12
Bonus Material
Separated Words

Some word pairs are meant to exist separately as two different words, some as single words, and some can be either way. Some, when used as two separate words, have a different meaning altogether. Consider the following examples:

Already vs. All ready
'Already' refers to something that has happened (probably ahead of time). 'All ready' means 'ready in all respects'. 'Already' is an adverb, whereas in 'all ready', 'all' is the intensifier for 'ready'.

I did not expect him so soon. He is here already.

Come anytime. I am all ready.

Altogether vs. All together
'Altogether' means 'completely'.

I could not altogether understand what you said.

'All together' refers to the grouping of all the people, objects, or events occurring at the same time or in one place.

Now, say all together—'Vande Mataram!'

'Altogether' may also mean 'in the nude'.

Anyone vs. Any one
Write 'anyone' as a single word, except while referring to a person or thing in a specific group.

All the sentences given below are correct:

Choose any one of the group as a mentor.

Anyone can learn English.

You cannot expect that anyone will be able to do it.

Anytime vs. Any time

'Anytime' is an adverb, whereas 'any time' is a noun phrase (adjective-noun combination).

He should be here anytime soon.

You can come in at any time.

Anyway vs. Any way

Use the phrase 'any way' for all cases, except when it means 'regardless' or 'in any case'.

Anyway, I was not planning to go to the party.

Go ahead and say what you want to. Anyway, I will do it my way.

Is there any way out?

Let us do it any way you want.

Anywhere is always anywhere

Inspector, you are welcome to search anywhere, except under the bed.

Awhile vs. A while

Both convey the same meaning, except that 'a while' takes a preposition.

I will sleep awhile.

I will sleep for a while.

Cannot vs. Can not

Both convey the same meaning, but 'cannot' is the more acceptable term in use.

Everyone vs. Every one

Use 'every one' for all cases, except when you can replace it with 'everybody'.

Everyone should attend.

Every one of you is going to receive a prize.

Sometime/Some time/Sometimes

'Sometime' is an adverb, and 'some time' is an adjective- noun combination. 'Sometimes' is always a single word. 'Sometime' means an indefinite moment in time; 'some time' denotes a period.

I will come sometime.

It will take me some time.

Sometimes, I get angry.

Everyday vs. Every day

'Everyday' is an adjective that means 'ordinarily' or 'normally'.

It was an everyday occurrence.

'Every day' is an adverb phrase meaning 'daily'.

Every day, I walk in the nearby park.

Whenever vs. When ever

'Whenever' is the standard form of usage. The same goes for 'however', 'whatever', 'whichever', 'whenever', 'wherever', and 'whoever'.

Whenever I ring the bell, no one answers.

There are special occasions when you can use 'when ever'.

When ever did I call you?

Whatever vs. What ever

'Whatever' is also used to express an absence of interest.

Mother (to teenager): 'You are coming with us, aren't you?'

Teenager: 'Whatever.'

What ever possessed you to act like that?

Exercise—Separate/joined words

Correct the following sentences, if required:

1. I am not sure when I'll be able to come. I'll be there some time.
2. It will take sometime for me to get ready.
3. Whatever the theme, the maiden sang, as if her song could have no ending.
4. When ever the bell rang, the dog salivated.
5. The problem is so simple that any one can do it.
6. Just call me any time.
7. Who so ever enters this gate is doomed.
8. I found that they were altogether in the conference hall.
9. I am altogether in agreement.
10. Hey, what's the hurry? Stay a while.

Answers—Separate/joined words

1. I am not sure when I'll be able to come. I'll be there sometime.
2. It will take some time for me to get ready.

3. What ever the theme, the maiden sang, as if her song could have no ending.
4. Whenever the bell rang, the dog salivated.
5. The problem is so simple that anyone can do it.
6. Just call me anytime.
7. Whosoever enters this gate is doomed.
8. I found that they were all together in the conference hall.
9. I am altogether in agreement.
10. Hey, what's the hurry? Stay awhile.

Weak Words

All forms of the verb 'be' can be weak. Examine the sentence where it occurs carefully to strengthen it. The following points need to be kept in mind:

- The verbs from the root 'be' are: am, are, is, was, were, been, and being.
- The various forms of the verb 'be' are static. They portray a state of 'being', not 'doing' and, hence, are inactive. If you overuse these forms, you will bore the reader.
- These verbs can be wordy.
- They often tell, not show.

Examples

(Original) The moon was among the clouds.

The 'was' here is static and weak. Note that it has no agency. Now, replace it with a stronger verb.

(Revised) The moon nestled amidst the clouds.

Another example:

(Original) The *dahi vada* is delicious.

(Revised) The *dahi vada* tastes delicious.

Don't you think this change has given the *dahi vada* some agency?

(Original) You should be writing every day.

(Revised) Write every day.

The revised version is less wordy.

(Original) I was hungry.

The above sentence seems concise and harmless. Now consider the following:

My stomach growled. I drooled at the sight of the *dahi vadas.*

Now you are showing rather than telling.

... Panju turned around and grabbed at the stick in the opponent's hand. The man tried to pull the stick back, but Panju held on. Panju let go of the stick suddenly and as the man staggered back, Panju leapt up in the air and kicked the man full in the face. The man dropped his stick, held his face and sat down, blood dripping between his fingers. The other man now came at him with his stick swinging. Dayalan was between the man and Panju. Panju grabbed Dayalan's arm at the elbow and applied pressure. Dayalan screamed in agony. The turbaned man followed him shortly afterwards, staggering a little....

In the above passage, quoted from my book, *Songs of the Cauvery*, in about 400 words, there is only one 'be' word.

When to use the various verb-forms of 'be'

Sometimes, the elimination of the 'be' verb makes the sentence longer. When you show rather than tell, it paints a picture before the reader's eyes, investing the sentence with importance. If you don't want the extra importance given by the showing, stick with the 'be' verb.

This can happen in fiction when you are telling a backstory or describing relatively unimportant characters—particularly with those who feature only once in the story.

Often, the use of these verbs is unavoidable. If a stronger verb exists or if showing improves the narrative, do it.

The following example is from the *Bhagavat Gita*, Chapter 1, Verse 20:

Gandiva (the bow) slips from my hand; my skins burns all over; I totter, and my mind reels.

This is instead of Arjuna saying — 'I am sad.'

Exercise—Eliminate the 'be' verbs

Eliminate the 'be' verbs from the following sentences:

1. She was upset with the news.
2. He was drunk and incoherent.

3. I should have been writing more often.
4. The book was on the table.
5. You should be eating what is on the plate.
6. She is walking very slowly.
7. What he should have done was to leave things alone.
8. He was eating; then he was walking.
9. It was a stupid thing that you did.
10. What she needed was a new scarf.
11. The warehouse was dark.
12. The man is lazy.

Answers—Eliminate the 'be' verbs

1. The news upset her.
2. He slurred.
3. I should write more.
4. The book lay on the table.
5. Eat what is on the plate.
6. She ambles.
7. He should have left it alone.
8. He ate; then he walked.
9. You did something stupid.
10. She needed a new scarf.
11. Shadows clung to every corner of the warehouse.
12. He sits all day long in the easy chair, sipping a beer and watching television.

Onomatopoeia

Onomatopoeic words sound like the noises they describe. Examples include 'hiss', 'rustle', or 'bang'.

Sensory words are words that describe the experience of the senses—sight, hearing, smell, feel, and taste.

Most words in the English language have their roots in Indo-European, Greek, and Roman languages. There are sensory words whose origin is based on certain syllables and phonemes, which, over time, have got associated with the sensory experience.

For example, the syllable 'gl-' has got associated with sight and light (glimmer, glimpse, glitter, etc.).

An important component of your style is your diction—choice of words. While describing something, attempt to build a strong image in the reader's mind, triggering associations through the choice of the right words.

Sensory words and onomatopoeic words help in this association.

> The plump blue-green bottle-fly settled on the concrete floor. I sat fascinated by the iridescent play of colours. I turned towards my son to share that appreciation. He calmly brought his foot down on the insect and squelched the fly underfoot.

The passage works because of the visual 'blue-green' and 'iridescent', the sensory 'plump', and the onomatopoeic 'squelching'.

A brief sampling of sensory and onomatopoeic words:

blast, buzz, chortle, clack, crackle, dazzle, dirty, fluffy, gargle, gloom, pound, scrape, shuffle, sight, slimy, smack, squelch, sticky, stomp, susurrate, tang, tinkle, trudge, whisper

Use onomatopoeic words. These make sense to the reader at a subliminal level.

Words often Confused

Lie vs. Lay

'Lay' as a transitive verb

A transitive verb takes an object; hence, 'lay', as a transitive verb, is to place something (the something being the object). You can lay something on the table.

Present: I lay everything down before I raise my hands.

Simple past: I laid the books on the table.

Past: (In the passive voice) The book was laid on the table.

Past continuous: I was laying the blanket on the bed.

'Lie' in the sense of 'to be in a flat position'

Note that this is an intransitive verb. You cannot lie something.

Simple present : I lie down to rest.

Simple past : He lay on the operating table for several minutes before the surgeon noticed him.

Past perfect (in the participle form) : He had lain on the bed for a very long time before he had fallen asleep.

'Lie' in the sense of uttering an untruth

Simple present: I lie as often as I can get away with.

Simple past: I lied. I didn't murder my boss.

Past participle: I had lied when I said that I didn't murder my boss.

The following table summarises the above:

	Lie (flat)	Lay (the blanket)	Lie (untruth)
Present tense	lie	lay	lie
Simple past	lay	laid	lied
Past participle	lain	laid	lied
Past continuous	lying	laying	lying

Exercise—Lie and lay

Correct the following sentences, if required:

1. Yesterday, the book laid on the table.
2. You lie to me yesterday; you lie to me today. Is there no end to your lies?
3. I lay senseless while I do not know what is happening all around me.
4. I lay senseless last Friday, even as the prayers were on.
5. I was laying the mattress on the bed that I wanted to lay on.
6. If I was tired, I would lay down on the couch.
7. She suggests that we all lay on the sand for a while.
8. I wish I had laid on the couch all day instead of working out.
9. I lie the book on the table (now).
10. I layed the book on the table yesterday.
11. I have lain the book on the table.
12. The book had laid on the table all day.

Answers—Lie and lay

1. Yesterday, the book lay on the table.
2. You lied to me yesterday; you lie to me today. Is there no end to your lies?
3. I lie senseless while I do not know what is happening all around me.
4. I lay senseless last Friday, even as the prayers were on.
5. I was laying the mattress on the bed that I wanted to lie on.
6. If I were tired, I would have lain down on the couch.

7. She suggests that we all lie on the sand for a while.
8. I wish I had lain on the couch all day instead of working out.
9. I lay the book on the table (now).
10. I laid the book on the table yesterday.
11. I have laid the book on the table.
12. The book had lain on the table all day.

Some more confusing words

Might have vs. May have
'Might have' is used to describe something that never really happened. 'May have' denotes a speculation about what happened.

They might have won the battle had they planned better.

(They did not win the battle.)

They may have won the battle, but they certainly lost the war.

(They probably won the battle.)

I vs. Me
When the pronoun (say, I) is the actor or the focus of interest, use 'I'. When the pronoun is acted upon or affected, use 'me'.

I bought a pair of socks.

Socks were bought by me.

Gokul and I are friends.

This has affected both Gokul and me.

Exercise—I, me

Correct the following sentences, if required:

1. 'I have this complaint,' she said. 'Me, too,' he said.
2. Chand and I are going to the movies tonight.
3. My student can write better than me.
4. Sonali gave both Ram and I dolls as gifts.
5. Both Ram and I were given gifts by Sonali.
6. Just between you and I, what is the truth?
7. She wanted my house more than I.
8. You and I make a great pair.
9. The whole world will blame this fracas on you and I.

10. There wasn't much in it for you or I.

Answers—I, me

1. 'I have this complaint,' she said. 'I, too,' he said. (Meaning, I, too, have the same complaint. While this is technically accurate, please note that mainstream usage has favoured 'Me, too.')
2. Chand and I are going to the movies tonight. (The sentence is correct.)
3. My student can write better than I. (This is another way of saying 'My student can write better than I can.')
4. Sonali gave both Ram and me dolls as gifts. (The pronoun is the object here.)
5. Both Ram and I were given gifts by Sonali. (The sentence is correct since 'I' is a subject here.)
6. Just between you and me, what is the truth? (Since the pronoun follows a preposition, it should be 'me'.)
7. She wanted my house more than me. (Both are right or wrong depending on the meaning you want to convey. If she preferred her house over me, then you should write 'me'. If she wanted the house more than I did, you should write 'I'.)
8. You and I make a great pair. (The sentence is correct as 'I' is a subject. Don't be misled by the fact that there are two subjects.)
9. The whole world will blame this fracas on you and me. (Note that the pronoun 'me' is preceded by a preposition, 'on'.)
10. There wasn't much in it for you or me. (Notice the preposition 'for' before the pronouns.)

Who vs. Whom (as relative pronouns)
Consider the following sentences:

He was the one whom we thought of as the leader.

He was the one who stole the cookies.

A simple way to determine whether 'who' or 'whom' should be used is to rewrite the sentence using a personal pronoun (he/she/they or him/her/them). If you need 'he', 'she', or 'they', use 'who'. If you need 'him', 'her', or 'them', use 'whom'.

Rewritten thus, the two sentences given above become:

We thought of him as the leader. (Therefore, use 'whom'.)
He stole the cookies. (Therefore, use 'who'.)

So, rewritten, the sentences above become:

Whom did we think of as the leader?
Who stole the cookies?

Exercise—Who, whom

Correct the following sentences, if needed:

1. I am hoping to meet the mystery writer, whom they say is a recluse.
2. We have always trusted our customers, who we figure, always tell the truth.
3. We have always checked with our customers, who we trust always.
4. Who did you see?
5. We will elect whoever promises more facilities.
6. We will elect whoever we can hold responsible.

Answers—Who, whom

1. I am hoping to meet the mystery writer, who they say is a recluse. (He, they say, is a recluse.)
2. We have always trusted our customers, who we figure, always tell the truth. (They, we figure, will always tell the truth.)
3. We have always checked with our customers, whom we trust always. (We trust them.)
4. Whom did you see? (I saw her.)
5. We will elect whoever promises more facilities.(He promises more facilities.)
6. We will elect whomever we can hold responsible. (We can hold her responsible.)

Its vs. It's

The apostrophe in 'it's' denotes that some letters are missing. 'It's' is the short form of 'it is' or 'it has'.

It's not correct. —> It is not correct.
It's been ten days since we met. —> It has been ten days since we met.

'Its' is the possessive form. (Note the absence of the apostrophe.)

The whale is a mammal, but its habitat is the ocean.

Exercise—Its vs. it's

Correct the following sentences:

1. Its our fate that we should see you every day.
2. It's trunk is curved in a strange manner.
3. Its true!
4. Its been several months since I ate a square meal.

Answers—Its vs. it's

1. It's our fate that we should see you every day.
2. Its trunk is curved in a strange manner.
3. It's true!
4. It's been several months since I ate a square meal.

For more words that are confused often, see Appendix 7.

Exercise—Words confused often

Correct, if needed, the following sentences:

1. This constant talk of war is aggravating me.
2. You should consider alternate systems of medicine.
3. The house which Biswas built is now crumbling.
4. Keep away from elephants that are angry.
5. What is your rationale for doing thus?
6. The principle method of dealing with the hungry is to feed them.
7. If you don't attack, you are going the loose the fight.
8. He had such a frightening experience. He literally drowned to death.
9. A separate vise squad was formed to combat crime.
10. The path was full of stones and brambles. The journey was indeed tortuous.
11. Don't tell me about the body in the basement. I am getting nauseous.
12. He was never arrested, though he was involved in a number of elicit enterprises.
13. Sen was a specially capable scientist.
14. Phoolan was famous for her misdeeds.

Answers—Words confused often

1. This constant talk of war is irritating me.

2. You should consider alternative systems of medicine.
3. The house that Biswas built is now crumbling.
4. Keep away from elephants that are angry.
5. What is your rationale for doing thus?
6. The principal method of dealing with the hungry is to feed them.
7. If you don't attack, you are going the lose the fight.
8. He had such a frightening experience. He nearly drowned.
9. A separate vice squad was formed to combat crime.
10. The path was full of stones and brambles. The journey was indeed torturous.
11. Don't tell me about the body in the basement. I am getting nauseated.
12. He was never arrested, though he was involved in a number of illicit enterprises.
13. Sen was an especially capable scientist.
14. Phoolan was notorious for her misdeeds.

Fun with Words

Here are some activities in which you could have fun with words and also feed your creative frenzy.

Neologisms

A neologism is a coined word or phrase. New definitions of existing words are also neologisms.

Change a letter

Coin your own words by adding, subtracting, or removing exactly one letter from an existing word, and give it a new definition.

Here are a few I have coined:

Vaccilation: Being undecided whether to get vaccinated.

Dentalist: A dentist who knows exactly which tooth is paining, without looking.

Factuary: A statistician who doesn't fiddle with facts.

Muddleaged: A confused period in one's life.

Blastphemy: The act of blowing up sacred religious monuments.

Nosetalgia: Remembrance of a smell long forgotten

Bibliopile: A book lover who enjoys seeing books all piled up haphazardly.

Writher: A writer who goes through torture while writing.

Coin your own portmanteau word!

A portmanteau is a word coined by blending existing words in such a way that the resulting word has a meaning that is a combination of their meanings.

Examples:

Brunch = breakfast + lunch

Chortle = chuckle + snort (Coined by Lewis Carroll)

Smog = fog + smoke

Spork = spoon + fork

Slithy = slithery + lithe

Mimsy = miserable + flimsy

Blurp = burp + slurp Or, a brief description on the back of a cookbook

Infracaninophile = infra + canine + phile—lover of the underdog (Coined by Christopher Morley)

Lewis Carroll made up a lot of nonsensical words in *Jabberwocky*.

Find new definitions to existing words

The following are from submissions to a neologism contest in the *Washington Post*.[2]

Coffee (N.), the person upon whom one coughs.

Flabbergasted (adj.), appalled over how much weight you have gained.

Abdicate (V.), to give up all hope of ever having a flat stomach.

Esplanade (V.), to attempt an explanation while drunk.

Pun to a template

Use the template, I used to work at <>—but I <>, to humorous effect.

I used to work in a blanket factory—I folded.

I used to work in a porcelain factory—I cracked up.

I used to work in a matches factory—I was burnt up.

I used to work in a soap factory—I was washed up.

---

2 https://carmamaths.org/resources/jon/Preprints/Oddments/werds.pdf for more.

I used to work in a library—I was booked.

I used to work in a fishery—I was hooked.

I used to work in a balloon factory—I blew up.

Now, roll your own…

Nine croans that will enlighten you

Croans are Zen-like questions or statements concerning a crow. If you meditate on these every day for three days or one year, whichever is shorter, you will get enlightened.

- What is the difference between a crow?
- Would a crow by any other name caw as loudly?
- If you meditate on a crow, will it get crushed?
- All crows are crows, except some.
- If you were the only crow in the world, would you still love other crows?
- If you removed the blackness from a crow, would it still be one?
- If you killed a single crow, would it be murder? What if it is married?
- If a crow caws in a forest, and there is no one to hear it, would you still be suspicious?
- What is the smell of one wing flapping?

Witty sayings from old ones

How to twist an existing saying:

Extend it to comic length

(Original) It cost an arm and a leg.

(Twisted) It costs an arm, a leg, a kidney, a liver, and an appendix.

Use similar words and re-metaphorise

(Original) An ounce of prevention is better than a pound of cure.

(Twisted) An ounce of contraception is better than seven pounds of delivery.

Top it by re-interpretation (use a surprise ending)

(Original) Ignorance is bliss.

(Twisted) Ignorance is bliss, but opinionated is better.

(Original) As alike as two peas in a pod.

(Twisted) As alike as two peas in a cloned pod.

Other examples

(Original) He was as busy as a bee.
(Twisted) He was as busy as a bee and twice as venomous.

(Original) He did not bat an eyelid.
(Twisted) He batted his entire forehead, eyes included.

(Original) Beware Greeks bearing gifts.
(Twisted) Beware geeks bearing gifts.

(Original) He was a big fish in a small pond.
(Twisted) He was a newly birthed tadpole in a small puddle.

Now, it is your turn.

1. The grass is always greener on the other side.
2. A bird in hand is worth two in a bush.
3. He was like a bull in a china shop.
4. A chip off the old block.
5. A face that only a mother could love.
6. A fool and his money are soon parted.
7. A hair of the dog that bit you.
8. A jack of all trades and master of none.
9. A leopard doesn't change its spots.
10. A man's home is his castle.
11. A penny saved is a penny earned.
12. A stitch in time saves nine.
13. Absence makes the heart grow fonder.
14. The apple doesn't fall far from the tree.
15. All roads lead to Rome.
16. Always the bridesmaid, never the bride.
17. Costs an arm and a leg.
18. Behind every great man, there is a great woman.
19. Blood is thicker than water.

Write a limerick

A limerick is a five-line poem with a rhyming scheme of AABBA—the first, second and fifth lines rhyme, and the third and fourth lines rhyme.

Lines 1, 2, and 5 are of 8/9 syllables, and Lines 3 and 4 are of 5/6 syllables.

Use a meter scheme of 3,3,2,2,3. The numbers are the number of stressed syllables—or 'dums'.

Lines 1, 2, and 5 go: da dum da dadum da dadum

Lines 3 and 4 go: da dum da dadum

Each of the lines is composed of anapaests.

(Anapaest is a metrical foot with three syllables—two unstressed syllables followed by one stressed syllable—as in, da dadum.)

Sample limerick

This is the first limerick in Edward Lear's *Book of Nonsense*.

There was an Old Man with a beard,

Who said, 'It is just as I feared—

Two Owls and a hen,

Four Larks and a Wren,

Have all built their nests in my beard!'

Another example:

There was a Young Lady of Dorking,

Who bought a large bonnet for walking;

But its colour and size,

So bedazzled her eyes,

That she very soon went back to Dorking.

EDWARD LEAR

Go on. Have fun. Write your own limerick. Make it funny.

A clerihew is simpler

A clerihew has four lines, rhyming couplets of AA, BB, a person's name as its first line, and something to say about that person in the subsequent lines. It should make you smile.

Sir Humphrey Davy
Abominated gravy.
He lived in the odium

Of having discovered Sodium.

Or,

Although Don Bradman
Screamed and fought like a madman
And condemned the proceedings in toto
They insisted on taking his photo.

ATTRIBUTED TO EDMUND CLERIHEW BENTLEY

Roll your own funny metaphors

Be inspired by PG Wodehouse in any of his books.

> *'Sad,' he sighed, 'that these idyllic surroundings should have become oppressed with a cloud of sinister menace. One thinks one sees a faun popping about in the undergrowth, and on looking more closely perceives that it is in reality a detective with a notebook....'*

PG WODEHOUSE, *LEAVE IT TO PSMITH*

PART 5:

ALL TOGETHER

Chapter 13
Structure and Patterns

Let's quickly go back to Rule 6 for a moment.

A story structure comprises a plot that you choose to tell, ordered in a particular way. You can order the events in multiple ways on different aspects of the story, creating diverse structures.

Even though I refer to the narrative as 'story', the patterns outlined are also applicable to non-fiction. You can incorporate good storytelling in non-fiction to, er, telling effect.

Increasing time

The ordering of the story can be that of strictly increasing time.

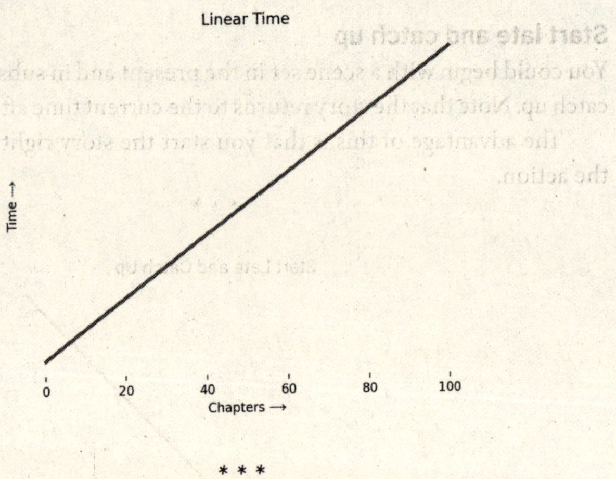

* * *

Back and forth in time

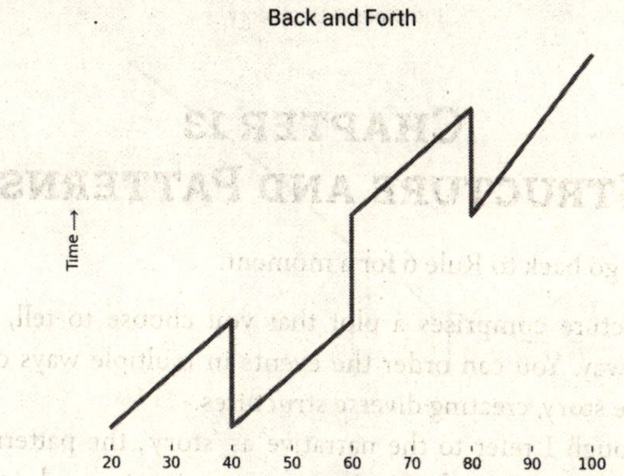

You could also wander back and forth in time (in alternate chapters, for instance). *A Man called Ove* by Fredrik Backman follows this structure.

* * *

Start late and catch up

You could begin with a scene set in the present and in subsequent chapters, catch up. Note that the story returns to the current time after a few chapters.

The advantage of this is that you start the story right in the middle of the action.

* * *

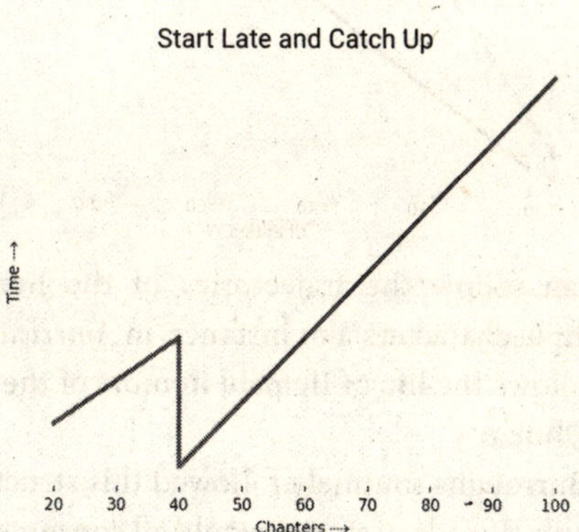

Intersperse backstory

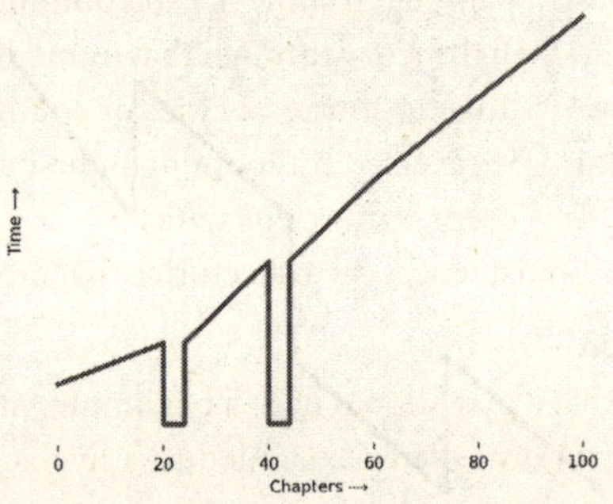

You can intersperse past scenes in small doses through the story so as to sustain the interest of the reader. This is often the preferred method.

Multiple characters

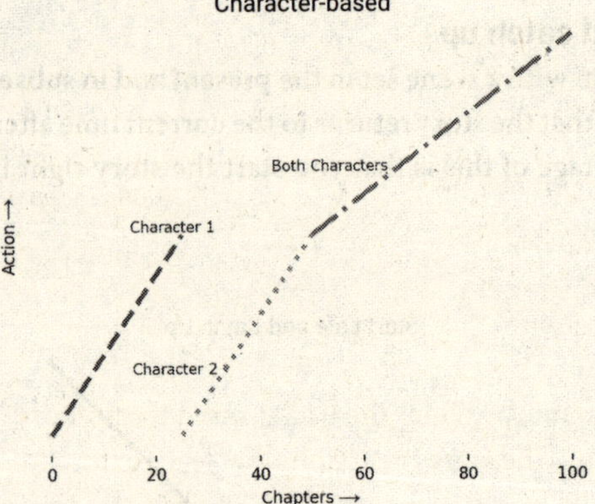

The story can follow the trajectories of the lives, thoughts, and emotions of multiple characters. For instance, in *Americanah*, Chimananda Nigazi Achebe follows the life of Ifemalu in most of the chapters but also has the POV of Obinze.

Edgar Rice Burroughs routinely followed this structure in his *Tarzan* novels. The multiple threads of stories would all converge later in the book.

Zoom in, zoom out

Another method, popular in non-fiction pieces, is to start with a zoomed out shot (descriptions), panning to show the surroundings and then zoom in to an individual and tell the story through that individual. Readers relate more to personal stories than to stories of cities or countries.

The order can also be reversed by zooming in first and describing the larger picture later. This order is more engaging.

I have just indicated a few of the trajectories that are possible.

Patterns of action

Aristotle believed that a play should have a beginning, middle, and an end. This three-act structure was later expanded to a five-act structure, as the diagram given below shows.

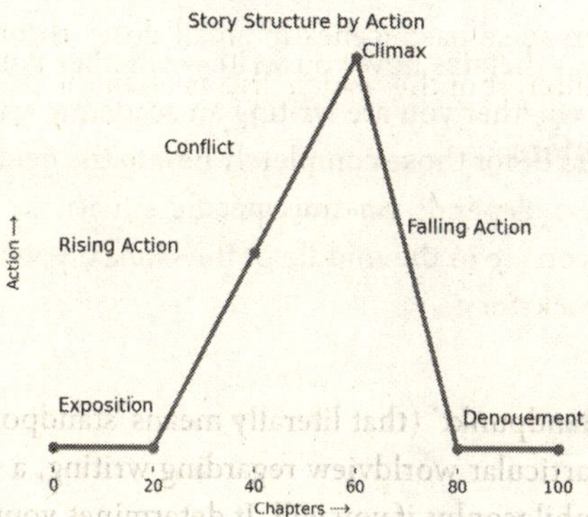

The five acts are:

Exposition: This provides the background to the story.

Rising action: These are the actions that lead to the climax of the drama. This part typically has an increasing level of obstacles for the protagonist.

Climax: This is the high point in the drama.

Falling action: The action slows down as all the twists in the plot are wrapped up.

Denouement or resolution: This is the final outcome of the drama.

Regardless of the structures or combinations you use, ensure that the reader's attention is consistently engaged.

CHAPTER 14
YOUR STANDPUNKT

Let's go back to Rule 10 for a while.

There has been a lot of pointed advice in these pages, some of it delivered as though you don't have a choice. The fact is that the option of how you write and whether you choose to follow a rule should depend upon not only the context but also your writing philosophy. These choices determine your writing style and voice.

Context

Who your reader is dictates how you write—whether you are writing for young readers or whether you are writing an academic article for grizzled veterans in the field or for those completely new to the field or for someone in-between. It also depends on the specific situational context in the narrative. When you are in the middle of the climax, you may not want to switch to a long backstory.

Standpunkt

I use the word 'Standpunkt' (that literally means 'standpoint' in German) to denote your particular worldview regarding writing, a well-considered personal writing philosophy, if you will. It determines your style.

There are often opposing forces that pull you in different directions. I believe that it is this creative tension that produces great literature. It is your Standpunkt and the context that determines your writing style. Let me enumerate some of these forces or the choices that you make.

Simple vs. Complex

Here is an example of the complex.

> *... First, with regard to certainty, I have pronounced judgment against myself by saying that in this kind of enquiries it is in no way permissible to propound mere opinions, and that everything looking like a hypothesis is*

counterband, that must not be offered for sale at however low a price, but must, as soon as it has been discovered, be confiscated.

IMMANUEL KANT, PREFACE TO THE *CRITIQUE OF PURE REASON*

This is not the stuff that you spring on young adults or even on someone who is looking for light entertainment.

Your style may be informal, and therefore, you gravitate towards simplicity. If you are doing some academic writing, the rules of the game that you follow are different.

The situational context also determines the simplicity or the extent of informality in the writing. A butler stereotypically spoke with formality and circumlocution. Here is Beach, the butler in Plum's *Summer Lightning*.

'Owing to the fact that you and Mr. Carmody have frequently entrusted me with your — may I say surreptitious correspondence — I have long been cognisant of your sentiments towards one another, miss. I am aware that it is your desire to contract a union with Mr. Carmody, and I knew that there would be objections raised on the part of certain members of the family.'

'So far,' said Hugo critically, 'this sounds to me like drivel of the purest water. But go on.'

PG WODEHOUSE, *SUMMER LIGHTNING*

Here is something simple but effective.

'Is that the mill?' he asked.

'Yes.'

'I do not remember it.'

'It was built since you were here. The old mill is farther down; much below the pass.'

He spread the Photostatted military map out on the forest floor and looked at it carefully. The old man looked over his shoulder. He was a short and solid old man in a black peasant's smock and gray iron-stiff trousers and he wore rope-soled shoes. He was breathing heavily from the climb and his hand rested on one of the two heavy packs they had been carrying.

'Then you cannot see the bridge from here.'

ERNEST HEMINGWAY, *FOR WHOM THE BELL TOLLS*

Plain vs. Lyrical

The voice that you use depends on your preference—whether you see yourself as a storyteller or stylist. You may even decide (on rare occasion) to use multiple voices in the same book. I did this in my book, *Songs of the Cauvery*.

I used a slightly lyrical voice while describing the Cauvery, which was not just a river but the thematic metaphor in the book.

> *The holy river Cauvery, daughter of gods, a gift to mankind, is born in an unassuming little tank at Tala Cauvery in the Western Ghats of South India. Were she to turn westwards, she would glimpse the handsome Arabian Sea. But that is not her lover and betrothed. He is eastwards, over 400 miles away. It is towards him that she must obsessively journey forth. At the source, she has the energy and the playfulness of youth. As she flows ahead, rushing recklessly through the hilly terrain, she is joined by her companions Harangi, Hemavati, Kabini and others, all daughters of the Western Ghats. She grows in confidence. She gushes forward, gathering not just the rich alluvia but also the culture, history and the stories of the lands around her, in turn influencing them.*

I used the voice of a historian to show the background of nationalism of the story.

> *In 1897, Bal Gangadhar Tilak wrote an article in the Kesari justifying the killing of Afzal Khan by Shivaji more than two hundred years before. He had written, 'God has not conferred upon the foreigners the grant, inscribed on a copperplate, of the Kingdom of Hindustan. The Maharaja (Shivaji) strove to drive them away from the land of his birth. He did not thereby commit the sin of coveting what belonged to others. Do not be circumscribed in your vision, like a frog in a well; get out of the Penal Code, and enter the extremely high atmosphere of the Srimad Bhagavad Gita, and consider the actions of great men.'*
>
> *The metaphorical allusion was not lost on the subtle Indian mind. On the twenty-second of June, the Collector of Poona, Mr. Rand, who was responsible for the plague measures, and a young military officer, Lt. Ayerst, were shot dead.*

The bulk of the rest of the story was in a different style.

> *It was an afternoon hour when, if the village of Tiruvaiyaru wasn't actually sleeping, it was definitely brimming with torpor. Mangalam stood in the inner courtyard in the middle of the house. The sky was darkening; a brown leaf on the packed earth swirled around and stopped; the musty smell of rain on fresh earth rose even before one or two spots of raindrops began to spread. For a moment, it awoke an automatic response within her. 'God, the clothes on the line at the back...' She smiled at the thought—a lopsided grin that didn't reach her eyes.*

The tension in your Standpunkt is the tension between form and content. You position yourself in such a way that the form does not drown out the content or vice versa. It is a deliberate and informed position that you should take. You may not be a professional poet like Michael Ondaatje but still sound lyrical without your message getting overpowered. Virginia Woolf, a stylist, does that in *Mrs. Dalloway.*

> *She would not say of anyone in the world now that they were this or were that. She felt very young; at the same time, unspeakably aged. She sliced like a knife through everything; at the same time, was outside, looking on. She had a perpetual sense, as she watched the taxi cabs, of being out, out, far out to sea and alone; she always had the feeling that it was very, very dangerous to live even one day. Not that she thought herself clever, or much out of the ordinary. How she had got through life on the few twigs of knowledge Fräulein Daniels gave them she could not think.*

VIRGINIA WOOLF, *MRS. DALLOWAY.*

Concise vs. Descriptive

When you show rather than tell, you normally need more words. What you lose in conciseness, you gain in engagement. I prefer to gain this engagement. At times, this may be an overkill. For instance, if you want a quick sketch, to reveal a bit of backstory, you may not want to have an entire scene devoted to it. Showing in a scene not only increases the engagement but also increases the importance of the backstory. This could set up an avoidable expectation in the reader's mind.

Compare:

He was mugged once.

To

His thoughts went back to that fateful day. He had been strolling aimlessly on Mass Avenue when at the corner of the 7th…

'Give me your mobile and whatever cash you have on you,' said the tall blond man with a scar running through his forehead and a knotted blue polka-dotted bandana round his neck…

You get the idea.

You also need to keep in mind the context. In the middle of a climactic scene, you cannot be describing the psychological motivations of an incidental character by creating, er…, a scene. You don't want to disrupt the pacing.

When the incident is vital to the plot and characterisation of the major characters, by all means, have a scene.

Here is evidence of something the master did not do. He did not delve into Claude Pott's childhood.

'What's self-respect got to do with it? There's nothing infra dig about snitching pigs. If I were differently situated, I'd do it like a shot. And I'm one of the haughtiest men in Hampshire.'

'Well, between you and me, Lord I.,' said Claude Pott, discarding loftiness and coming clean, 'there's another reason. I was once bitten by a pig.'

'Not really?'

'Yes, sir. And ever since then I've had a horror of the animals.'

Lord Emsworth hastened to point out that the present was a special case.

'You can't be bitten by the Empress.'

'Oh no? Who made that rule?'

'She's as gentle as a lamb.'

'I was once bitten by a lamb.'

Lord Ickenham was surprised.

PG WODEHOUSE, *UNCLE FRED IN THE SPRINGTIME*

Short vs. Long sentences

Short, simple sentences lend a pace to the writing and absorb the reader in the story rather than lose him in the prose.

However, a very long sequence of short sentences may bore the reader. You need variety. You need a long sentence here and there to break up the staccato rhythm of short sentences.

The sentences don't have to be long and complicated to lend a unique style to your writing.

Look at the length of the sentences in Kurt Vonnegut's *Slaughterhouse-Five* and the variation.

Billy survived, but he was a dazed wanderer far behind the new German lines. Three other wanderers, not quite so dazed, allowed Billy to tag along. Two of them were scouts, and one was an antitank gunner. They were without food or maps. Avoiding Germans, they were delivering themselves into rural silences ever more profound. They ate snow.

They went Indian file. First came the scouts, clever, graceful, quiet. They had rifles. Next came the antitank gunner, clumsy and dense, warning Germans away with a Colt.45 automatic in one hand and a trench knife in the other.

SLAUGHTERHOUSE-FIVE, BY KURT VONNEGUT

You also have writers like James Joyce who wrote a 4000 + word sentence in *Ulysses*.

I prefer to err on the shorter side, while varying the length of the sentences. What about you?

Direct vs. Tangential

Write for a careful and intelligent reader. This means that you can communicate through:

- things left unsaid
- body language
- metaphors and symbolism

In the following passage from *Songs of the Cauvery*, for example, Krishna Iyer's wife subtly denies the imputation that she is responsible for them being childless.

Thus, when Krishna Iyer from a well-known dubashi family from Madras proposed that he would adopt Vichu and ensure that he completed his education, he jumped at the offer. Krishna Iyer had said, 'I don't think we have any chance of a son,' all the while looking at his wife, who was busy looking at her toes, shaking her head almost imperceptibly, attempting passively to deny the imputation of her husband's glance.

I prefer leaning on the side of subtlety, not euphemism. When the reader figures out something you have not stated explicitly, he gets a special type of joy. Give it to him.

Your style would vary depending on where you position yourself under the influence of such opposing forces.

Conciseness vs. Repetitiveness

Sometimes, depending upon who your reader is, you may have to repeat some information for emphasis or for better absorption. This redundancy should be a choice and should not happen without you being aware of it. The resulting text may be longer and seem superfluous, but that is a deliberate choice. You may also repeat to get a desired cadence. (See Anaphora and Epistrophe under rhetorical devices.)

Less is more vs. More is more

It is better if the reader infers from what you write—to just leave the dots in and let the reader connect them. This has a side effect of making the writing more concise. On the other hand, your reader may be a young reader for whom you need to spell things out.

If you explain every motivation, the reader might get bored. Readers, particularly of genre fiction, do enjoy the occasional incursion into a character's head and the resulting interior monologue.

General vs. Specific

It is much better to be specific. Rather than shooting someone down with a gun, you should have your assassin use an FN FNS longslide 9mm handgun that has a 17-round magazine. Rather than the character visit some place for some unknown purpose, let her visit Bangalore for the specific purpose of eating her favourite food, mushroom toast, at Koshy's on St. Mark's Road.

It means more words, but it is worth the cost if the event is significant to the story or to the character development. You don't need to state that a casual bystander spat on the road because of childhood trauma and go into specifics.

Conclusion

Where you place yourself on these various dimensions and others depends on your own writing philosophy and the specific context. This becomes the determinant of your unique style. Also, even though there might be a writerly recommendation, understand the 'why' of the 'writing rules' and follow them faithfully before you break them.

PART 6: RESOURCES

Appendix 1
(Transition Words)

- next, later, meanwhile, subsequently
- similarly, in the same way, likewise
- in contrast, yet, even so, alternatively, but, however, nevertheless, nonetheless, on the contrary, although, while
- above all, in particular, indeed
- accordingly, so
- for example, for instance, in other words, that is
- for this reason, for this purpose
- as a result, in consequence, therefore, thus
- in short, once again, to repeat
- of course, surely, certainly, after all
- in sum, as we have seen, on the whole, all in all, more important (ly)
- on the other hand, therefore, so, consequently, despite this, paradoxically, etc.

Appendix 2 (Tautologies)

Use the word in brackets instead of the redundant phrase.

- actual fact (fact)
- final conclusion (conclusion)
- in order to (to)
- surrounded completely on all sides (surrounded)
- completely unique (unique)
- interact with each other (interact)
- as to whether (whether)
- congregate together (congregate)
- shuttle back and forth (shuttle)
- close proximity (proximity)
- summarise briefly (summarise)
- added bonus (bonus)
- false pretences (pretences)
- general vicinity (vicinity)
- past history (history)
- plan ahead (plan)
- return back (return)
- gather together (gather)
- sufficient enough (sufficient)
- close proximity (repetition)
- completely eliminate (eliminate)
- end result (result)
- basic fundamentals (fundamentals)
- collaborate together (collaborate)
- final outcome (outcome)
- brief summary (summary)
- repeat again (repeat)

Appendix 3 (Figures of Speech/Rhetoric)

Allegory

Allegory is a story that has a hidden story within. The characters and the events in the story are symbolic of something else.

Examples:

Animal Farm by George Orwell is a commentary on social dynamics. It talks of freedom, equality, and the struggle for power—through animal characters.

Gulliver's Travels by Jonathan Swift is a criticism of British policies of that time.

The Lord of the Rings by J. R. R. Tolkien is symbolic of the struggle between good and evil.

Allusion

An allusion is a brief reference to a well-known piece of literary work. It can refer to a person, place, thing, event, or other literary work with which the reader is presumably familiar.

'Hey, be back by midnight to avoid your car turning into a pumpkin.' This is a reference to the fairy tale, *Cinderella*.

'He shimmered in like Jeeves.' This is a reference to a popular character created by PG Wodehouse.

Be careful with allusions, because they can date you. There is a possibility of you alluding to something that is not commonly known and switching off the reader, unless you are James Joyce.

If you write 'She stood over the trapdoor, looking like Marilyn Monroe on the grate', not only will you date yourself but also probably lose your audience.

Analogy

Analogy is the comparison between two situations, objects, etc., usually for a clearer understanding.

The atom is like a miniature solar system. The nucleus is the sun and the planets are the electrons.(For a moment, disregard the fact that it is a false analogy.)

Analogies also have comedic potential.

Explaining a joke is like dissecting a frog. You understand it better, but the frog dies in the process.

EB WHITE

Anaphora

Anaphora is the repetition of a word or a group of words at the beginning of clauses or sentences that follow each other. This is more a rhetoric than a literary device. The repeating words are used for setting up a cadence and an emphasis, as in Churchill's:

'We shall fight on the beaches, we shall fight on the landing grounds, we shall fight in the fields and in the streets, we shall fight in the hills; we shall never surrender.'

A Tale of Two Cities opens with an anaphora:

It was the best of times, it was the worst of times, it was the age of wisdom, it was the age of foolishness, it was the epoch of belief, it was the epoch of incredulity, it was the season of Light, it was the season of Darkness, it was the spring of hope, it was the winter of despair.

CHARLES DICKENS, *A TALE OF TWO CITIES*

Epistrophe

Epistrophe is the repetition of words at the end of clauses or sentences.

In the famous Gettysburg speech, Lincoln says:

... That these dead shall not have died in vain–that this nation, under God, shall have a new birth of freedom and that government of the people, by the people, for the people, shall not perish from the earth.

ABRAHAM LINCOLN, GETTYSBURG SPEECH

Note the repetition of 'the people', lending both cadence and emphasis.

Anthropomorphism

Anthropomorphism is the treatment of a non-human being as though possessing the characteristics of a human being.

Example:

The animals in George Orwell's *Animal Farm* talk and plot against humans.

Anthropomorphism is a literary device in which a non-human object or character behaves the way a human would act or otherwise exhibits the characteristics of a human being. Use this literary device with animal characters or even with non-living, inanimate objects.

At this moment, the laurel bush, which had hitherto not spoken, said 'Psst!' The butler started violently. A spasm went through his frame. 'Beach!' said the bush.

PG WODEHOUSE, *SUMMER LIGHTNING*

Asyndeton

It is a literary device in which some conjunctions are omitted while joining sentences or clauses. This creates a sense of urgency and immediacy.

An example is the Latin *'Veni, vidi, vici'* and its translation into English—I came, I saw, I conquered. (Not—I came, saw, and conquered.) Note the anaphora in the repetition of the 'I'.

I recommend you don't overuse this in written prose as it can sound overdramatic.

Hyperbole

Hyperbole is an exaggeration. When combined with a metaphor or simile, it can be effective. Humorous writers often use hyperbole.

Nature, stretching Horace Davenport out, had forgotten to stretch him sideways, and one could have pictured Euclid, had they met, nudging a friend and saying: 'Don't look now, but this chap coming along illustrates exactly what I was telling you about a straight line having length without breadth.'

PG WODEHOUSE IN *UNCLE FRED IN THE SPRINGTIMES*

Plum was also the master of the understatement. Consider:

Anybody who was content to call you fairly good-looking would describe the Taj Mahal as a pretty nifty tomb.

PG WODEHOUSE IN *THE CLICKING OF CUTHBERT*

Juxtaposition

Juxtaposition is a literary device in which two concepts are placed close to each other so that the reader can compare and contrast them.

One man's meat is another man's poison.

Ask not what your country can do for you, ask what you can do for your country.

JOHN F. KENNEDY

Malapropism

The origin of the word lies in a character's name—Mrs Malaprop in Sheridan's play, *The Rivals*. She often used the wrong word, using one that sounded like the apt word. So, this wrong use of one word for the other (particularly one that sounds like the correct one) is a malapropism.

This example is from the play.

She's as headstrong as an allegory on the banks of the…

RICHARD BRINSLEY SHERIDAN, *THE RIVALS*

She meant to say 'alligator'.

Onomatopoeia

When a word is formed with the sound it is associated with, you have onomatopoeia.

Example: cuckoo, buzz, hiss, bang, trill, cough, roar

Onomatopoeic verbs help in forming powerful imagery.

'The bug was squelched' evokes a more powerful image than 'the bug was killed'.

See also a separate section on onomatopoeia.

Personification

Personification is the attribution of human characteristics to non-human beings or objects.

Anthropomorphism, as discussed earlier, is a special case of personification where animals are invested with human characteristics.

A number of personifications are used in everyday speech.

My feet are killing me.

My laptop died on me.

In poetry, personification is very common. For instance:

Death, be not proud, though some have called thee

Mighty and dreadful, for thou art not so;

For those whom thou think'st thou dost overthrow

Die not, poor Death, nor yet canst thou kill me.

JOHN DUNNE, *DEATH BE NOT PROUD*

Terry Pratchett, in his *Discworld* series, goes a step beyond and makes a character out of Death.

Here is a personification of Nature from Plum.

Blandings Castle slept in the sunshine.... It was that gracious hour of a summer afternoon, midway between luncheon and tea, when Nature seems to unbutton its waistcoat and put its feet up.

PG WODEHOUSE, *SUMMER LIGHTNING*

Portmanteau words

As explained earlier, these are multiple words combined to create a new word.

Examples:

Spoon + fork = spork

Frappe + cappuccino = Frappuccino

Bombay + Hollywood = Bollywood

Brother + romance = bromance

Breakfast + lunch = brunch

Satire

In satire, human foibles and vices are held up in ridicule with humour, irony, and exaggeration. Satire is both a genre and the means of ridiculing human vices.

Examples include Jonathan Swift's *Gulliver's Travels,* Aldous Huxley's *Brave New World,* and Orwell's *Animal Farm.*

Symbolism

Symbolisms are literary devices. They use symbols, such as marks, people, or abstract ideas, to represent a distinct reality.

In *The Kite Runner* by Khaled Hosseini, the kite serves as the symbol of the protagonist's ambitions, as well as guilt. In *The God of Small Things*, Arundhati Roy uses several symbols—Rachel's watch, Pappachi's moth, etc.

Rahel's toy wristwatch had the time painted on it. Ten to two. One of her ambitions was to own a watch on which she could change the time whenever she wanted to (which, according to her, was what Time was meant for in the first place).

ARUNDHATI ROY, *THE GOD OF SMALL THINGS*

In *The Lord of the Rings*, 'The One Ring' is a symbol of power and selfishness.

Synesthesia

Synesthesia is a rhetorical/literary device that uses one sense for the other. Hearing a colour, smelling a sound, or seeing a smell are all examples of synesthesia.

The crimson red tore at my eyes.
My love is blue.

Or,

O, for a draught of vintage! that hath been
Cool'd a long age in the deep-delved earth,
Tasting of Flora and the country green,
Dance, and Provençal song, and sunburnt mirth!

JOHN KEATS, *ODE TO A NIGHTINGALE*

Transferred epithet

This is a device in which an adjective of a noun (normally used to qualify the noun) is transferred to another noun.

I had a sad day at the office.

Here, the day is not sad; I am. The adjective 'sad' is transferred to 'day'.

April is the cruellest month, breeding
Lilacs out of the dead land, mixing
Memory and desire, stirring
Dull roots with spring rain.

TS ELLIOT, *WASTELAND*

A transferred epithet can also be used to comic effect, and PG Wodehouse is a great wielder of such an effect.

> *As I sat in the bath-tub, soaping a meditative foot and singing, if I remember correctly, 'Pale Hands I Loved Beside the Shalimar', it would be deceiving my public to say that I was feeling boomps-a-daisy.*

APPENDIX 4 (COMPLEX WORDS)

Simpler words

- Use 'say' instead of 'utter'.
- Use 'happy' instead of 'pleased'.
- Use 'good' instead of 'beneficial'.
- Use 'bad' instead of 'detrimental'.
- Use 'easy' instead of 'facile'.
- Use 'hard' instead of 'arduous'.
- Use 'fast' instead of 'speedy'.
- Use 'slow' instead of 'leisurely'.
- Use 'hot' instead of 'scorching'.
- Use 'walk' instead of 'ambulate'.
- Use 'happy' instead of 'euphoric'.
- Use 'big' instead of 'monstrous'.
- Use 'drink' instead of 'imbibe'.
- Use 'said' instead of 'uttered'.
- Use 'small' instead of 'petite'.
- Use 'talk' instead of 'converse'.
- Use 'happy' instead of 'elated'.
- Use 'scared' instead of 'petrified'.

For further examples, look up:[3]

Filler words

- well
- so
- you know
- basically

3 https://www.plainlanguage.gov/guidelines/words/use-simple-words-phrases/

- honestly
- anyway
- actually
- seriously
- clearly
- obviously
- definitely
- absolutely
- honestly
- essentially
- honestly
- literally
- virtually
- honestly
- technically
- right
- I mean
- okay
- alright
- sure
- I guess
- I think
- sort of
- kind of
- really
- truly
- honestly
- in fact
- of course
- just
- simply
- well
- actually
- especially
- particularly

- frankly
- needless to say
- in any case
- by the way
- to be honest
- believe me
- as I was saying
- all in all

APPENDIX 5
(VAGUE WORDS)

'Very' words

Here is a list of some 'very' words and their feasible alternatives.

- very angry > furious (enraged, incensed, livid)
- very roomy> spacious
- very quiet > noiseless
- very new> novel
- very nervous > apprehensive
- very negative > pessimistic
- very necessary > essential
- very neat > immaculate
- very neat > orderly
- very near > handy
- very hot > scorching
- very cold > frigid
- very big > gigantic
- very small > tiny
- very fast > speedy
- very slow > sluggish
- very sweet > sugar-coated
- very sour > tart
- very dry > arid
- very wet > drenched
- very clear > transparent
- very dirty > filthy

Appendix 6
(Adverb Replacement)

Strong verbs instead of adverbs

- ran quickly > sprinted
- spoke loudly > shouted
- ate quickly > devoured
- looked carefully > scrutinised
- worked hard > toiled
- laughed loudly > guffawed
- walked quietly > tiptoed
- sang beautifully > serenaded
- moved slowly > crept
- smiled happily > beamed
- talked loudly > bellowed
- ate noisily > slurped
- ran fast > bolted
- looked closely > examined
- worked diligently > laboured
- laughed heartily > roared
- walked slowly > sauntered
- sang loudly > belted
- moved quickly > darted
- smiled warmly > grinned
- talked rapidly > jabbered
- ate greedily > wolfed down
- ran eagerly > charged
- looked intently > stared
- worked efficiently > streamlined
- laughed uncontrollably > cackled
- walked briskly > strutted

- sang passionately > crooned
- moved stealthily > slinked
- smiled mischievously > smirked
- talked confidently > asserted
- ate ravenously > feasted
- ran smoothly > glided
- looked curiously > peered
- worked meticulously > crafted
- laughed infectiously > giggled
- walked gracefully > sashayed
- sang melodiously > harmonised
- moved gracefully > swayed
- smiled slyly > sneered

APPENDIX 7
(MORE WORDS OFTEN CONFUSED)

I have given below some more words that are often confused. In the examples, I have shown the corrected usage following the wrong usage. In the third line, I have given the correct usage of the wrongly used word.

Acronym/Initialism

An acronym is pronounced as though it is a word, and an initialism is spelt out. Thus, UNESCO is an acronym (for United Nations Educational Scientific and Cultural Organization) and FBI, an initialism, as it is spelt out as F-B-I.

(Wrong) UFO is an acronym for Unidentified Flying Objects.

(Corrected) UFO is an initialism for Unidentified Flying Objects.

(Correct) SETI is an acronym for Search for Extraterrestrial Intelligence.

Aggravate/Irritate

'Aggravate' is to make an already bad situation worse; 'irritate' is to annoy, whether or not the person was already annoyed.

(Wrong) Don't aggravate me. I am reading.

(Corrected) Don't irritate me. I am reading.

(Correct) Don't aggravate the wound. It will fester.

Alternate/Alternative

An 'alternative' is something that you can use instead of something else. 'Alternate' is to swing between two different states.

(Wrong) An alternate method is to try calming them down.

(Corrected) An alternative method is to try calming them down.

(Correct) Have you noticed how these bands of colour alternate?

Amount/Number

'Number' refers to countable things; 'amount' is used for things that are not countable.

(Wrong) What is the amount of cigarettes you have smoked?

(Corrected) What is the number of cigarettes you have smoked? (Better still: How many…)

(Correct) The amount of harm cigarettes can cause is huge.

Apprise/Appraise

'Apprise' is to inform someone; 'appraise' is to judge someone or something.

(Wrong) I will appraise Holmes that you are waiting.

(Corrected) I will apprise Holmes that you are waiting.

(Correct) I am not going to appraise all the jewellery.

Auger/Augur

'Auger' is a tool; 'augur' is to portend something.

(Wrong) This war does not auger well for the world.

(Corrected) This war does not augur well for the world.

(Correct) I will use an auger for cleaning this hole.

Bemused/Amused

'Bemused' is to be confused and unable to think clearly; 'amused' is to think something is funny. Sadly, 'bemused' is one of those words that has received the right to be used in the meaning of 'amused' due to repeated wrong usage.

(Wrong) I was bemused by the humour in his words.

(Corrected) I was amused by the humour in his words.

(Correct) I was bemused at the thought that I would have to write a difficult examination the next day.

Beside/Besides

'Besides' means 'apart from'; 'beside' means 'by the side of'.

(Wrong) Beside me, no one knew the truth.

(Corrected) Besides me, no one knew the truth.

(Correct) He has been beside me, through thick and thin.

Biennial/Biannual/Semi-annual/Bimonthly

'Biennial' is once in two years. 'Biannual' and 'semi-annual' mean twice a year. Unfortunately, 'bimonthly' can mean both once in two months and twice a month. Avoid its usage.

Take/Bring

Both imply a movement of an object. 'Bring' is used when the object is moved nearer to the speaker/actor. 'Take' is used when the object is moved farther.

(Wrong) When you are coming to Bangalore, you must take your clothes with you.

(Corrected) When you are coming to Bangalore, you must bring your clothes with you.

(Correct) Take this coat when you are going to England.

Canvas/Canvass

'Canvas' is a kind of cloth and 'to canvass' is to solicit, say, for votes.

(Wrong) I plan to stand for the post of vice-president in the club elections. Will you canvas votes for me?

(Corrected) I plan to stand for the post of vice-president in the club elections. Will you canvass votes for me?

(Correct) I watched fascinated, as the artist started to stretch his canvas.

Childish/Childlike

Both mean resembling a child. 'Childish' has a negative connotation; 'childlike' is positive. You could call immature behaviour 'childish'. You can admire the 'childlike' innocence of someone.

(Wrong) What I like about her is her childish innocence.

(Corrected) What I like about her is her childlike innocence.

(Correct) Don't ever play such childish pranks on me.

Chord/Cord

'Cords' are strings and 'chords' are a combination of musical notes. When you talk of the voice box, you should be talking about vocal cords and not vocal chords.

(Wrong) Don't strain your vocal chords by singing loudly.

(Corrected) Don't strain your vocal cords by singing loudly.

(Correct) His talk struck a deep chord in me.

Classical/Classic

'Classic' is something of lasting value—it can also mean 'typical'. 'Classical' is something that relates to antiquity or long tradition.

(Wrong) That was a classical joke.

(Corrected) That was a classic joke.

(Correct) You must study the classical writings of the Greeks and the Romans.

Climatic/Climactic

'Climatic' relates to climate and 'climactic' relates to climax.

(Wrong) Global warming will be accompanied by other climactic changes.

(Corrected) Global warming will be accompanied by other climatic changes.

(Correct) In the climactic scene, the villain initially points the gun at the hero, then reverses it and shoots himself.

Complement/Compliment

A 'complement' is something that fulfils a part; a 'compliment' is a word or words of praise. Something 'complimentary' can also be something that is free.

(Wrong) He said I am not bad looking. I consider that a complement.

(Corrected) He said I am not bad looking. I consider that a compliment.

(Correct) Her physical strength complemented my intelligence.

Comprehensive/Comprehensible

'Comprehensive' means 'with complete coverage'; 'comprehensible' is 'that which can be understood'.

(Wrong) He was slurring. He was barely comprehensive.

(Corrected) He was slurring. He was barely comprehensible.

(Correct) The book on writing was comprehensive. It covered practically everything under the sun.

Comprise/Compose

'Comprise' is 'to consist of'; 'compose' is 'to be formed with various parts'.

(Wrong) The group comprises of six people.

(Corrected) The group is composed of six people.

(Correct) The group comprises six people. (Please note it is not 'comprised of'.)

Continual/Continuous

'Continuous' means 'without stopping'; 'continual' means 'recurring'.

(Wrong) The viral fever has been in this town continuously since 1886.

(Corrected) The viral fever has been in this town continually since 1886.

(Correct) He has been circling the Earth continuously for three months.

Denote/Connote

'Denotation' is what a word directly and literally signifies, and 'connotation' is the indirect implication.

The same word could denote something and also connote something else.

(Wrong) Blue connotes a colour.

(Corrected) Blue denotes a colour.

(Correct) Blue may connote a sad mood.

Discreet/Discrete

To be 'discreet' is to be unobtrusive; 'discrete' means 'separate'.

(Wrong) Jeeves was in many ways a discrete butler.

(Corrected) Jeeves was, in many ways, a discreet butler.

(Correct) Light can even be conceived as consisting of discrete particles.

Credible/Credulous/Creditable

'Credible' means 'believable'. 'Credulous' describes someone who is trusting. 'Creditable' means 'praiseworthy'.

(Wrong) The articles in *Daily Crime* are not creditable. They are meant for the credible public.

(Corrected) The articles in *Daily Crime* are not credible. They are meant for the credulous public.

(Correct) The chess master did a creditable job of training the nation's young.

Deduce/Deduct

'Deduce' means 'to infer'; 'deduct' means 'to subtract'.

(Wrong) Holmes was able to deduct from a sample of hair that the boy was twelve, an orphan, and loved cake.

(Corrected) Holmes was able to deduce from a sample of hair that the boy was twelve, an orphan, and loved cake.

(Correct) You seem to have deducted a lot of money from my salary. What was that for?

Disinterested/Uninterested

'Disinterested' is to be impartial; 'uninterested' is to be not interested. A judge should be disinterested but not uninterested. However, these days, you can get away with using 'disinterested' instead of 'uninterested'.

(Wrong) This boy has eaten so much junk food that he is disinterested in regular food.

(Corrected) This boy has eaten so much junk food that he is uninterested in regular food.

(Correct) An umpire needs to be disinterested.

Enervating/Energising

'Enervating' is 'weakening' and 'energising' is to 'add energy'.

(Wrong) Thank you for your enervating talk.

(Corrected) Thank you for your energising talk.

(Correct) After hearing the sad news, she felt enervated.

Entitled/Titled

'Titled' refers to the name of a book, song, etc. 'Entitled' is what a person has a right to. 'Entitled' is used as a verb. When used as an adjective, it may refer to an attitude of a person who feels he has a claim to a lot of things in life.

(Wrong) I have written a fantasy novel entitled 'The Sorcerer of Mandala'.

(Corrected) I have written a fantasy novel titled 'The Sorcerer of Mandala'.

(Correct) You are entitled to your opinion.

(Correct) The child was spoilt and grew up to be an entitled youth.

Exceptionable/Exceptional

'Exceptionable' means 'open to objection'; 'exceptional' is 'outstanding'.

(Wrong) I think the CEO of my company is exceptionable.

(Corrected) I think the CEO of my company is exceptional.

(Correct) Some rules in my company are exceptionable to a large extent.

Exercise/Excise/Exorcise

'Exercise' is to 'work the muscle'; 'excise' is to 'remove'; and 'exorcise' is to 'get rid of ghosts'.

(Wrong) Let me exercise the entities that possess you.

You certainly don't want to exercise a ghost! Ectoplasmic ones are bad enough; a muscular one will be too much.

(Corrected) Let me exorcise the entities that possess you.

(Correct) Exercise makes you stronger.

(Correct) The surgeon excised the tumour.

Fictional/Fictitious

'Fictional' is relating to a story; 'fictitious' is 'a made-up lie'.

(Wrong) Professor Moriarty is my favourite fictitious character.

(Corrected) Professor Moriarty is my favourite fictional character.

(Correct) That is completely fictitious. I did not steal that gold bullion.

Fortuitously/Fortunately

'Fortuitously' is 'by chance' (good or bad); 'fortunately' is 'through (good) luck'.

(Wrong) I was fortuitous enough to get a million dollars in the lottery.

(Corrected) I was fortunate enough to get a million dollars in the lottery.

(Correct) That change in my job was entirely fortuitous. I had nothing to do with it.

Further/Farther

While multiple shades of meaning are possible, I suggest you use 'farther' for physical distance and 'further' to mean 'moreover' or 'additionally'.

(Wrong) I will go no further than ten kilometres.

(Corrected) I will go no farther than ten kilometres.

(Correct) I have nothing further to say on this topic.

Hanged/Hung

'Hanged' refers to a human being; 'hung' refers to an inanimate object or dead being.

(Wrong) He was hung by the official hangman.

(Corrected) He was hanged by the official hangman.

(Correct) The picture hung crooked.

Healthy/Healthful

Technically, people are 'healthy' and foods can be 'healthful', but like many things that become the norm after repetitive usage, 'healthy' can be used for foods that are 'healthful' as well.

Historical/Historic

'Historical' means 'pertaining to history', whereas 'historic' is used for significant moments in history.

(Wrong) The Dandi march was a historical moment in the subcontinent's history.

(Corrected) The Dandi march was a historic moment in the subcontinent's history.

(Correct) Historical records are often written by the victor.

Imply/Infer

When A means something without stating directly and B deduces something from it, A is 'implying' and B is 'inferring'.

(Wrong) Forgive me if I inferred in any way that you are a bloody fool.

(Corrected) Forgive me if I implied in any way that you are a bloody fool.

(Correct) I infer from your talk that the butler must have done it.

Insignificant/Nonsignificant

'Insignificant' means 'trivial'. 'Nonsignificant' is something to which no significance can be attached.

(Wrong) The statistical analysis showed that gender is insignificant.

(Corrected) The statistical analysis showed that gender is nonsignificant.

(Correct) 'Sire,' said the minister, 'I feel insignificant in front of you.'

Less/Fewer

Use 'fewer' for countable items and 'less' for others.

(Wrong) Make less mistakes.

(Corrected) Make fewer mistakes.

(Correct) The food I was getting at the hostel was less than what I was used to.

Like

It is used in the sense of errors, like grammar mistakes.

Consider the sentence:

Spelling mistakes like this should not be made.

The implication is that you could make other mistakes, even spelling mistakes, not resembling this. Better to say:

'Spelling mistakes such as this should be avoided.'

Literally/Nearly

'Literally' means 'actually'. It cannot be used in the sense of 'almost' or 'nearly'.

(Wrong) I literally drowned in the tub.

(Corrected) I nearly drowned in the tub.

(Correct) That was literally true. He actually did drown in the tub.

Loose/Lose

'Loose' means 'not tight'. 'Lose' is 'to fail to keep something'.

(Wrong) If you keep telling the truth, you are going to loose the case.

(Corrected) If you keep telling the truth, you are going to lose the case.

(Correct) The shirt was so loose that it flapped in the wind.

Marital/Martial

'Martial' relates to war; 'marital' relates to marriage.

(Wrong) The tunes of the marital music made me want to march.

(Corrected) The tunes of the martial music made me want to march.

(Correct) I declined to attend the wedding. I just sent a message wishing them all marital bliss.

Misinformation/Disinformation

'Misinformation' may or may not be deliberate, whereas 'disinformation' is always so.

(Wrong) She fell prey to the misinformation campaign and hated her president.

(Corrected) She fell prey to the disinformation campaign and hated her president.

(Correct) By the time I wanted to act, it was too late. The misinformation had spread.

Ordinance/Ordnance

'Ordinance' is a formal government order; 'ordnance' is military hardware.

(Wrong) Emperor Jehangir had issued a dozen ordnances.

(Corrected) Emperor Jehangir had issued a dozen ordinances.

(Correct) The ordnance factory smelt of cordite.

Poured/Pored

'Pour' is 'to make a fluid substance flow'. 'Pore' is 'to delve deeply into the written material'.

(Wrong) She poured over her books till late at night.

(Corrected) She pored over her books till late at night.

(Correct) She hated herself because she had just poured coffee all over her books.

Prone/Supine

'Prone' is lying face-down. 'Supine' is lying down on one's back.

(Wrong) He lay prone. A big gash could be seen on his forehead.
(Corrected) He lay supine. A big gash could be seen on his forehead.
(Correct) After the eye surgery, she was advised to lie prone.

Purposefully/Purposely

'Purposefully' means 'with a lot of purpose and aim', whereas 'purposely' means 'deliberately'.

(Wrong) After winning the argument, the alien strode purposely from the room.
(Corrected) After winning the argument, the alien strode purposefully from the room.
(Correct) He lost the argument purposely.

Rational/Rationale

'Rational' means 'logical'. 'Rationale' is a reason for a course of action, belief, or decision.

(Wrong) What is your rational for behaving like this?
(Corrected) What is your rationale for behaving like this?
(Correct) No rational person would have behaved thus.

Rein/Reign

An emperor 'reigns' (rules); you 'rein' in (stop by pulling on the reins) a horse.

(Wrong) Krishnadevaraya reined over a large kingdom.
(Corrected) Krishnadevaraya reigned over a large kingdom.
(Correct) He reined his horse in just as they had reached the river.

Rob/Steal

You 'rob' an establishment but 'steal' an object.

(Wrong) He robbed a watch from his employee.

(Corrected) He stole a watch from his employee.

(Correct) He robbed a retail outlet of a famous branded watch.

Sensual/Sensuous

'Sensual' refers to someone who loves physical pleasures, particularly sex. 'Sensuous' refers to someone or something that is pleasing to the senses.

(Wrong) 'Don't give in to your sensual pleasures,' said the yogi, on seeing the student caress his muslin robe.

(Corrected) 'Don't give in to sensuous pleasures,' said the yogi, on seeing the student caress his muslin robe.

(Correct) She thrilled in the almost sensual feel of the sweet in her mouth.

Simple/Simplistic

'Simple' means plain and clear and 'simplistic' is treating complex problems as though they were simple.

(Wrong) She didn't want to choose a simplistic dress.

(Corrected) She didn't want to choose a simple dress.

(Correct) The solution he had offered was simplistic.

Stationery/Stationary

'Stationery' stands for items related to writing and other office materials. 'Stationary' means 'not moving'.

(Wrong) The van was stationery when the truck hit it.

(Corrected) The van was stationary when the truck hit it.

(Correct) We had a special blackhole in the office wherein a number of stationery items disappeared, never to be seen again.

Torturous/Tortuous

'Torturous' means inducing torture; 'tortuous' means winding.

(Wrong) The first few weeks of training were tortuous.

(Corrected) The first few weeks of training were torturous.

(Correct) So far, we were travelling on a straight line, but now the tortuous path lay ahead of us.

Venal/Venial

'Venal'means bribable, corrupt; 'venial' means small sins that don't get you to hell.

(Wrong) The venial customs officer confiscated a bottle of whisky.

(Corrected) The venal customs officer confiscated a bottle of whisky.

(Correct) Lying may not be a venial sin; it can get you into trouble all the same.

Verbal/Oral

'Verbal' may refer to anything spoken or in writing, and 'oral' refers to something only spoken.

(Wrong) She did extremely well in the oral segment of the test.

(Corrected) She did very well in the verbal segment of the test.

(Correct) The scriptures were all transmitted orally.

Vice/Vise

'Vice' refers to criminality involving sex or drugs; 'vise' is a tool with jaws for gripping an object. Please note that the British spelling for 'vise' can be 'vice'.

(Wrong) Even though it looked innocuous from outside, the building was really a den of gambling and vise.

(Corrected) Even though it looked innocuous from outside, the building was really a den of gambling and vice.

(Correct) I could not free myself from her vise-like grip.

Which/That

'That' introduces restrictive clauses and 'which', non-restrictive ones.

(Correct) The elephant that belongs to the temple is considered sacred.

Here, 'that belongs to the temple is considered sacred' answers the question, 'which elephant?' It refers to a restricted class of elephants—those that belong to the temple.

(Correct) The elephant, which is a gentle being, is fond of sugarcane.

(Note the comma after 'elephant' that is mandatory after non-restrictive clauses.)

Here, 'which is a gentle being' is just a description—a bit of additional information. It does not serve the purpose of narrowing the possible list of elephants. It applies to all elephants.

The following sentences are all correct:

The building that has a gargoyle is the one that is haunted.

The *Bhagavat Gita* is a book that every one needs.

The two sentences preceding do not convey the intended sense without the clause including 'that'.

The dog, which responded well to kind treatment, is now safe.

The car, which was dirty from smoke and pollution, stopped at the street lights.

In these two sentences, the intended sense is conveyed by using 'which'.

Please note that the use of 'which' in this sense is preceded by a comma—in fact, the entire clause is set off within commas.

At times, you may omit 'that' for stylistic reasons, as in:

The *Bhagavat Gita* is a book everyone needs.

Use 'who' instead of 'that' for individuals and 'that' for inanimate objects and groups.

The man, who seemed familiar, spoke Arabic.

Men that are wicked at heart may receive punishment in the afterlife.

The pen that stopped writing leaked.

Wringer/Ringer

'Wringer' is a piece of equipment for twisting clothes and removing excess water. 'Ringer' is a device or person that rings a bell.

(Wrong) By the time I finished the run, I felt as though I had been through a ringer.

(Corrected) By the time I finished the run, I felt as though I had been through a wringer.

(Correct) We had five more minutes of torture in the classroom as the official ringer was late in ringing the bell.

Wrought/Wreaked

'Wrought' refers to a metal that has been formed by hammering or a change that has been effected. 'Wreaked' refers to an event or a person that has caused a lot of damage.

Don't use 'wrought' as a past tense or past participle of 'wreak'. 'Wrought' is the archaic form of 'worked'.

(Wrong) The cyclone had wrought damage all along the coast.

(Corrected) The cyclone had wreaked damage all along the coast.

(Correct) The figurine was crude, but was wrought from a single piece of metal.

You're/Your

'You're' means 'you are'. 'Your' is what belongs to you. (In simpler words, it is the second person possessive determiner.)

(Wrong) You're diction is excellent.

(Corrected) Your diction is excellent.

(Correct) You're going to be in a lot of trouble if you don't perform.

Appendix 8
Resources for the Writer

Motivation

The following books can provide you the motivation to start or continue writing:

1. Anne Lemont, *Bird by Bird: Some instructions on Writing and Life.* This has both practical advice, encouragement, and motivation for the writer.
2. Steven Pressfield, *The War of Art: Break Through the Blocks and Win Your Inner Creative Battles.* This book is about overcoming the resistance that writers and other artists often face when creating their work. It is a great book for any artist, including a writer.
3. Stephen King, *On Writing: A Memoir of the Craft.* This book is a memoir and writing advice from King. He writes on the writing process and provides practical tips for improving your craft.

Writing fiction

Books on fiction-writing

1. Noah Lukeman, *The First Five Pages: A Writer's Guide to Staying Out of the Rejection Pile.* Among other things, the book discusses the importance of the first few pages of the manuscript.
2. *The Writer's Digest Handbook of Novel Writing*, edited by the Editors of Writer's Digest. This is a comprehensive guide on all aspects of novel writing.
3. John Gardner, *The Art of Fiction: Notes on Craft for Young Writers.* This is a comprehensive book on writers starting out on their literary journey.
4. William Strunk Jr. and E.B. White, *The Elements of Style.* This is a classic guide to writing style. It is a must-read for any fiction writer. It covers the basics of grammar, punctuation, and word choice.

Websites/blogs for fiction writers

1. The Writing Cooperative: https://writingcooperative.com/
2. Writers Digest: https://www.writersdigest.com/
3. The Write Practice: https://thewritepractice.com/
4. The Write Life: https://thewritelife.com/

Podcasts for fiction writers

1. Writing Excuses (https://writingexcuses.com/): This podcast is hosted by a group of authors.
2. The Creative Penn (https://www.thecreativepenn.com/podcasts/): This podcast is hosted by a bestselling author.

Books for some genres

Mystery and crime fiction: This genre includes works of fiction that revolve around solving a crime or mystery. Examples include detective novels, mystery novels, and thrillers.

1. Nancy J. Cohen, *Writing the Cozy Mystery*
2. Sue Grafton et al., *Writing Mysteries*
3. Barry Turner, *The Writer's Handbook Guide to Crime Writing*
4. James N. Frey, *How to Write a Damn Good Mystery*
5. Martin Edwards, *Howdunit: A Masterclass in Crime Writing by Members of the Detection Club*

Romance: This genre includes works of fiction that focus on romantic relationships and the emotional interactions between characters. Examples include romantic comedies, historical romances, and contemporary romance novels.

1. Leigh Michaels, *Writing the Romance Novel*
2. M.L. Buchman, *The Romance Writer's Pink Pages: The Insider's Guide to Selling Your Romance Novel*
3. Julie Beard, *The Complete Idiot's Guide to Getting Your Romance Published*

Science fiction and fantasy: This genre includes works of fiction that take place in a futuristic or otherworldly setting and may involve elements of science fiction or fantasy. Examples include science fiction novels, fantasy novels, and dystopian novels.

1. Crawford Kilian, *Writing Science Fiction and Fantasy*
2. James Gunn, *The Science of Science-Fiction Writing*
3. Orson Scott Card, Philip Athans, and Jay Lake: *Writing Fantasy & Science Fiction: How to Create Out-of-This-World Novels and Short Stories*
4. Ray Bradbury, *Zen in the Art of Writing. The Fantasy Writer's Handbook*
5. Ursula K. Le Guin, *Words Are My Matter*

Horror: This genre includes works of fiction that are intended to scare or horrify the reader. Examples include horror novels, supernatural thrillers, and gothic fiction.

1. Stephen King, *Danse Macabre*
2. Edited by Mort Castle, *Writing Horror: A Handbook by the Horror Writers Association*

These are just a few examples of the many different genres of fiction that exist. There are many other genres, such as historical fiction, westerns, and graphic novels, to name a few.

Books on non-fiction writing

These books cover a range of topics related to non-fiction writing, including style, structure, research, and the business of writing.

1. William Zinsser, *On Writing Well: The Classic Guide to Writing Nonfiction*
2. Sue William Silverman, *Fearless Confessions: A Writer's Guide to Memoir*
3. Dinty W. Moore, *The Truth of the Matter: Art and Craft in Creative Nonfiction*

Websites for non-fiction writers

These websites offer information and resources for non-fiction writers, including tips, techniques, and guidance on how to improve your skills and succeed as a non-fiction writer.

1. The Nonfiction Writers Conference: https://nonfictionwritersconference.com/
2. The Creative Nonfiction Foundation: https://www.creativenonfiction.org/
3. The Memoir Network: https://www.thememoirnetwork.com/

Books on screenwriting

1. David Trottier, *The Screenwriter's Bible*
2. Blake Snyder, *Save the Cat!*
3. Robert McKee, *Story: Style, Structure, Substance, and the Principles of Screenwriting*

Websites for screenwriters

1. The Black List: https://www.blcklst.com/
2. The Script Lab: https://thescriptlab.com/
3. The Writers Guild of America: https://www.wga.org/

Screenwriting software

1. Final Draft: This is a professional screenwriting software used by many screenwriters.
2. Scrivener: This is a multi-purpose writing software that is popular with many writers, including screenwriters.
3. Celtx: This is a free, cloud-based screenwriting software.

Editing

Books on editing

1. Renni Browne and Dave King, *Self-Editing for Fiction Writers*
2. Claire Kehrwald Cook, *Line by Line: How to Edit Your Own Writing*
3. James Scott Bell, *Revision and Self-editing*
4. Browne and King (2004), *Self-Editing for Fiction Writers*
5. Susan Bell (2007), *The Artful Edit*

Style manuals

1. University of Chicago Press: The Chicago Manual of Style. This is a widely-used style guide that covers grammar, style, and usage and is an essential resource for writers and editors.
2. The Associated Press Stylebook (https://www.apstylebook.com/): This website is a widely-used style guide for journalists, with information on grammar, style, and usage.

Software for editing

1. Grammarly (https://www.grammarly.com/)
2. ProWritingAid (https://prowritingaid.com/)

3. The Hemingway App (https://www.hemingwayapp.com/): This website is a tool that helps writers improve the clarity and concision of their writing.
4. ChatGPT (https://openai.com/)
5. Claude (https://claude.ai/)

Book formatting

Books for formatting

1. Joel Friedlander, *The Self-Publisher's Ultimate Resource Guide*

Websites for formatting

1. The Book Designer (https://www.thebookdesigner.com/)

The following are self-publishing platforms that include a comprehensive guide to formatting ebooks and print books.

1. Smashwords (https://www.smashwords.com/books/view/52)
2. Reedsy (https://www.reedsy.com/)
3. Createspace (https://www.createspace.com/en/resources/book-formatting)
4. KDP (https://kdp.amazon.com/en_US/help/topic/G200672640)

Grammar, punctuation, and usage

Books for grammar and usage

Apart from the manuals of style, the following books will be useful:

1. Mignon Fogarty, *Grammar Girl's Quick and Dirty Tips for Better Writing*
2. Roy Peter Clark, *The Glamour of Grammar: A Guide to the Magic and Mystery of Practical English*
3. Lynne Truss, *Eats, Shoots & Leaves*: *The Zero Tolerance Approach to Punctuation*
4. Benjamin Dreyer: *Dreyer's English: An Utterly Correct Guide to Clarity and Style*

Online dictionaries

1. Merriam-Webster Dictionary (https://www.merriam-webster.com/)

2. The Oxford English Dictionary (https://www.oed.com/)
3. Dictionary.com (https://www.dictionary.com/)
4. The American Heritage Dictionary (https://www.ahdictionary.com/)
5. Cambridge Dictionary (https://dictionary.cambridge.org/)

Online Thesauruses

1. Merriam-Webster Thesaurus (https://www.merriam-webster.com/thesaurus)
2. Thesaurus.com (https://www.thesaurus.com/)
3. https://www.wordhippo.com/
4. Oxford Thesaurus of English (https://www.oed.com/thesaurus)
5. Cambridge Thesaurus (https://dictionary.cambridge.org/thesaurus/)

Online reverse dictionaries

A reverse dictionary is a type of reference tool that allows you to search for words based on their definition rather than by their spelling or pronunciation. This can be useful for writers who are looking for the right word to use in a particular context.

1. WordHippo Reverse Dictionary (https://wordhippo.com)
2. OneLook Reverse Dictionary (https://www.onelook.com/reverse-dictionary.shtml)
3. Thesaurus.com (https://www.thesaurus.com/browse/reverse%20dictionary)

Software for book design

1. Adobe InDesign: This is a professional-grade design software that is commonly used by publishers and designers to create books, magazines, and other print materials.
2. Vellum: This is a Mac-only book formatting and design tool that makes it easy to create professional-looking ebooks and print books.

It is important to choose a software program that meets your needs. You may also want to consider whether you need a program that is specifically designed for creating books or if a more general-purpose design or word processing program (like MS Word or Scrivener) will suffice.

Acknowledgements

To Anita Nair for her valuable suggestions.

To Sundari Bala Francis for meticulously reviewing an early draft.

To Dr Karthik Kalyanaraman for providing important suggestions on the structure of the book.

To Divyanka George Thambuswamy, Rohan Roberts, D. Sampath, Dr Shiv Sastry, Pawan, Pratima Rao, and Rugmani Prabhakar for reading an early draft and providing helpful input.

To The Bangalore Writers Collective for their motivation.